Fine Tuning Your Three-Point Attack:
150 Concepts to Improve Any
Team's Three-Point Offense

- Kevin Sivils -

*"Kevin Sivils's books should be required reading for coaches! I'm always impressed by the shear number of solid, time-tested and thought-provoking ideas he presents, giving the reader a "one-stop shopping" resource. In **Fine Tuning Your Three-point Attack** he has great suggestions not only for coaching the shooter, but the concepts and drills you need to be aware of generate open looks from the arc. His section on quick-hitters, sideline and underneath OB plays alone are worth the price of the book, and will help you make the three-point shot an integral part of your offense!"*

> Coach Doug Porter – Head Women's Basketball Coach Olivet Nazarene University – National Collegiate Scoring Champions

"His thought provoking approach makes for an easy read and will definitely stimulate thought and, most likely, change the way you go about coaching offense."

> Rusty Rogers – Two-time NAIA Division II Women's Basketball National Championship Coach and Two-time NAIA National Coach of the Year

"Coach Sivils does an outstanding job of breaking down the individual components, skills, and base blocks of being an efficient and effective 3-point shooter, then putting the pieces back together to highlight the impact of the 3-point shot and how it continues to shape the game today."

> Daniel Koutsis - Assistant Men's Basketball Coach Calumet College

"Coach Sivils clearly brings his experience in the game of basketball to his writing. He is a great teacher who acquire great gifts over the years and it's great he wants to share those gifts with other coaches."

> Bill Reidy – Long time successful High School and AAU Basketball Coach

"Prolific basketball author Kevin Sivils provides another soup to nuts scoring guide. While at its core, offensive basketball is a game of cutting and passing, Coach Sivils helps players and coaches achieve their full potential SHOOTING the basketball. The three-point rule revolutionized basketball over thirty years ago, and "Fine Tuning" presents an advanced treatise on the benefits, limitations, and mechanics of enhancing your perimeter game."

Ron Sen, MD, - Middle School Basketball Coach

"When it comes to player development, there is nothing more important than the coach's knowledge of fundamentals and details. Coach Sivils provides expert advice for coaches desiring to develop that essential knowledge base."

Jeremy Donalson – High School Basketball Coach

"For the coach who wants to take full advantage of the 3-point shot on offense, this book is a great resource for ideas about maximizing the offensive value of the 3-point shot."

James Rodgers – High School Basketball Coach

"I was surprised at the broad coverage of information included in the book. If there is a kitchen sink in basketball, Coach Sivils has thrown it in this book."

Matt Dodger – High School Basketball Coach

"The value of this book is not any earth shaking new offensive ideas for obtaining 3-point shots or how to shoot the three, though I did learn new ideas, it is having all of this information gathered in one place."

Bill Janssen – High School Basketball Coach

"Coach Sivils provides meticulous shooting fundamentals for my middle schoolers to prepare them for the challenges of shooting at the high school level. The style of offense will make for a fun, uncommon style of play at the middle school level."

Andrew Collazo – Middle School Basketball Coach

Fine Tuning Your Three-Point Attack:

150 Concepts to Improve Any
Team's Three-Point Offense

Kevin Sivils

A Southern Family Publishing

KCS Basketball Enterprises, LLC
Katy, Texas

Fine Tuning Your Three-Point Attack:
150 Concepts to Improve Any Team's Three-Point Offense

Photography by David Shutts of
Shutts Photography

Photography by Maddy Copello

Published by *A Southern Family Publishing*

A Division of KCS Basketball Enterprises, LLC

www.kcsbasketball.com

Using This Book

Like other books in the *Fine Tuning Series*, the information presented is not meant to be a comprehensive system of 3-point offense and shooting. It is meant to be a guide, a source of ideas and inspiration, to improving what you as a coach already do on offense in regards to utilizing the 3-point shot as an offensive weapon.

I am a firm believer in a coach doing what feels comfortable and fits with his or her system of play. Simply adopting wholesale what another coach does will work sometimes but more often than not problems will result. This is due to the coach adopting the system and not having the personnel to execute the system or ultimately the coach does not believe in several of the core principles of the system.

Either way, problems will crop up. Coaching legend Don Meyer told coaches repeatedly at his summer Bison Basketball Camps "you can get all the good ideas, you just can't use them all." What great advice for any coach, veteran or rookie regardless of the level of play.

If what you are doing works for you and your program, there is no need to throw the baby out with the bathwater. *Fine Tune* your system! Take the ideas presented in this book that fit your players, your system and your beliefs in how the game should be played and use these concepts to fine tune, to improve, what you are already doing. Save the rest of the ideas for when your program is faced with a big change in personnel or for whatever reason, you feel your system is in need of a complete makeover.

Some of the information presented may not seem like it is directly related to 3-point shooting or offense. What does starting, stopping and turning have to do with 3-point offense? Everything if you ask John Wooden and the coaches who follow his philosophy of teaching fundamentals. Specialists in biomechanics will confirm everything starts with the feet and the base of balance and support established with the feet.

Why is the fact every zone defense turns into a 2-3 zone when the ball is moved to the corner relevant to 3-point offense? Because a 2-3 zone is vulnerable to particular offensive building blocks, the screen-in tactic for example, that are particularly effective if setting up good, open 3-point shots.

If you have a firm grasp on how to integrate the 3-point shot into your existing offensive system, this book may help you iron out any kinks in the system or provide you with small insights that will help you develop your players into better 3-point offensive weapons.

I have used every concept presented in this book successfully during my 20+ seasons as a varsity head coach and have used these concepts regardless of the tempo or style of play a given team used that season. Fast breaking teams can benefit from using these concepts as much as deliberate, half court teams.

Some of the concepts in this book are repeated in other books I have authored. This is because I believe these concepts are so important they need to be repeated as often as possible. They include the importance of the team concept, teaching fundamentals and for coaches to not tolerate sloppy execution of basic skills.

If you are interested in building a complete system of play utilizing as the center focus of the offense the 3-point shot and have more questions, please contact me using the information on the *Contact the Author* page. Consider asking me questions and receiving an answer as part of the purchase agreement for this book.

A Note About Systems of Shooting

In a book about offense, particularly 3-point offense, a word needs to be said about shooting. Let's face it, you can have the best ideas in the game about how to obtain good 3-point shots for your players, but if none of your players are able to shoot the ball from 3-point range with any degree of accuracy or consistency, then all the ideas are of little value.

The focus on this book is to help coaches develop a systematic approach to developing an offense that makes full use of the benefits of the 3-point shot. As such, shooting is part of that approach but a bit beyond the scope of what this book is intended to accomplish. There are several key principles all systems have in common. Rather than advocate a specific system of shooting in this book, the general principles common to all successful shooting systems will be mentioned and explained.

Programs that produce great shooting teams season after season do not do so by accident. The coaches who lead these programs utilize well developed and thought out systems of shooting and methods to teach and practice these systems.

No one particular system of shooting will be advocated in this book, though I have studied and used several during my 20+ years of coaching. To name a few, I have studied the Don Eddy System, the Dick Baumgartner System as well as the teachings of Coach Don Meyer.

All of these approaches to teaching shooting have merit and will produce players who are capable of consistently excellent shooting. Like everything else, these systems have their drawbacks.

It is wise to keep the following in mind when looking for a system of shooting to adopt. There is more than one way to skin a cat. Which method will work best for you and your players?

Contents

Concepts and Drills for Practicing the 3-Point Shot 101

Fast Break 3-Point Drills: 111

Building Block/Footwork 3's: 115

Secondary Breaks for the 3-Point Shot 121

1

The Case for the 3-Point Shot

The 3-point shot is an accepted part of the game at all levels of play now. It was a bit controversial when the rule was first implemented, requiring coaches to rethink the logic of how they taught offense. The math involved is still relevant today and bears repeating so coaches can understand different ideas about how to implement the 3-point shot and why what is sometimes considered conventional wisdom does not apply.

For starters, let's examine the traditional means of evaluating shooting, field goal percentage. Teams, or individual players, who shoot at or close to 50% from 2-point field goal range are considered to be excellent shooters and to possess excellent shot selection. This standard of measurement has not changed.

Using this long held unit of measurement for excellence in 2-point shooting as a guide, how is good 3-point shooting measured statistically? Using 100 shots from 2 @ 50% = 100 pts. as the standard, what is an equivalent field goal percentage for the 3-point shot? The basic equivalent would be 100 shots from 3 @ 33% = 99 pts.

Just what does this mean from a statistical perspective? Simply this, you do not have to shoot the same percentage from 3-point range to be as effective.

The 3-point shot has changed the game in other ways as well. Good 3-point shooters and 3-point shooting teams force defenses to extend further from the goal, creating more space for the offense. This single factor was the most important reason the rules committee had for adopting the 3-point shot.

More space for the offense means the defense will have greater difficulty in stopping penetration via the dribble or pass, doubling on offensive post players and clogging the interior of the court, making it difficult to obtain the desired high percentage 2-point shots.

Yet another advantage of the 3-point shot is the longer rebounds missed field goal attempts. This negates to a limited degree the advantage of size in the rebounding phase of the game. Smaller, quicker players can run down the longer rebounds, allowing them to compete with the larger, slower players who traditionally dominated the rebounding phase of the game due to size and the short distance from the rim that rebounds traveled.

The 3-point shot has reintroduced skill, hustle and speed as significant factors in the game of basketball. No longer is sheer size, brute strength and athleticism the only factors capable of dominating a game. The 3-point shot has been good for the game. It is here to stay.

2

What the 3-Point Game Can Do

Running the regular offense will work just fine. Why make specific changes to accommodate the 3-point shot? Why focus on certain fundamental skills to better take advantage of the 3-point shot? After all, the three is only one part of the game of basketball!

If it takes a little convincing to see the need to integrate the 3-point shot into your regular offense and develop players who can take advantage of 3-point shot opportunities, consider the following eight concepts:

- Score in big surges
- To a point, you are never out of a game
- Create opportunity to catch up in a hurry
- Open up the offense
- Create driving opportunities
- Change how teams defend you
- Creates a fun style of play for the players
- Creates a fun atmosphere for the fans

Score in Big Surges

Basketball is a game of momentum. The 3-point shot can play a large role in shifting or creating momentum. For example, if the opponent scores six points by making three consecutive 2-point goals, this can create some momentum. If your team responds with a pair of consecutive 3-point goals, not only has the six points been matched, the manner in which it was accomplished can not only negate the opponent's momentum but transfer it to your team.

Because three points are rewarded for a made 3-point field goal, making three or four 3-point shots in a short time span scores more points than a comparable number of made 2-point shots. The extra points from the 3-point field goals create a surge in scoring that can snowball into a run of unanswered points.

To a Point, You Are Never Out of a Game

There is a point where a team is so far behind it becomes unlikely the team will be able to score enough points to catch-up and take the lead. With the 3-point shot, the number of points a team can fall behind and still catch-up becomes greater.

The ability to create momentum, surges and long unanswered runs with by using the 3-point shot makes it possible for teams to stay in games longer and make a comeback even after falling behind by a considerable margin. To put it a different way, large leads are no longer safe.

Create Opportunity to Catch up in a Hurry

When trailing in a game, time is always the enemy. The 3-point shot allows more points to be scored for the same number of shots taken from 2-point field goal range, increasing the speed with which a deficit can be overcome. Combine the increased scoring from 3-point range with the surges and runs the 3-point shot can create, an amazing number of points can be scored in a short period of time.

Open Up the Offense

With proper spacing, which is always a key component of good offensive play, the 3-point shot will open up the offense, creating more scoring opportunities for post players, penetration and general balanced scoring opportunities for all players.

Create Driving Opportunities

The 3-point shot when combined with good offensive spacing forces the defense to extend further from the goal than many defensive teams would like, creating larger gaps in the defense and increasing the distance defenders must travel to provide help against penetration. The effect of spreading the defense thereby increasing the distance between defenders, creates larger attack lanes for offensive players to dribble penetrate to either score or create scoring opportunities for teammates.

Change How Teams Defend You

Teams will be forced to alter their normal strategy and tactics in defending an excellent 3-point offensive team. Teams who normally prefer to play a "pack" style of man-to-man defense, clogging the lane and making post play difficult, will be forced to extend their defense, opening the lane and making post defense more difficult. Teams who prefer to play a "push" style of aggressive denial man-to-man defense will have to dial back their pressure or be overly vulnerable to dribble penetration. Zone defense teams may have to play man-to-man defense due to the large gaps now created in the zone defense.

Creates a Fun Style of Play for the Players

The 3-point shot is a fun part of the game. It encourages players to develop their skills in order to take advantage of the shot. Players who can shoot the 3-point shot must develop the ability to penetrate and score as well as the ability to penetrate and pass. Post players must not only be able to score inside but now must be able to find and pass to open perimeter shooters. The increased scoring opportunities, often combined with an up tempo pace make the game exciting and fun to play!

Creates a Fun Atmosphere for the Fans

Basketball is a spectator sport. Large, vocal crowds make the game more fun for players, fans and coaches. The 3-point shot, with its ability to create surges in scoring, momentum changes and creating the possibility the team who is behind can always come back, makes the game more interesting and entertaining for the fans. The shot itself is exciting when a player scores from such a distance from the goal and when combined with other plays in the game of basketball such as the give and go, the fast break or the dunk, it is one more component of the game that makes it so fan friendly.

3

Problems With the 3-point Shot

Nothing in life is perfect and the 3-point shot is no different. Being aware of potential problems allows a coach to prepare for the inevitability of these issues cropping up and to have a way to deal with each of these challenges. Some players seem to think if a few 3-point shots are a good thing then certainly a lot of 3-point shots are even better. Some issues requiring advance planning include:

- You can shoot yourself out of a game
- Can create shot selection problems
- Decrease in free throw opportunities
- Perimeter lapses
- Stagnant offense

You Can Shoot Yourself Out of a Game

The 3-point shot can create large scoring surges and changes in momentum. It can also create large scoring surges for the opponent when a drought from beyond the 3-point line occurs, erasing large leads in short periods of time. Players must be aware of the rules of shot selection, time and score, the need for balance in the type of shots taken and the type of shots to work for when a 3-point drought takes place.

Can Create Shot Selection Problems

Shot selection is a difficult enough concept to teach players. It includes issues such as a player's ability to shoot a specific shot, time and score, the need to control tempo and the need to take high percentage shots. When teaching shot selection it is essential to include the 3-point shot and all the concepts of what makes a good 3-point shot opportunity. When all else fails, shot restrictions, the practice of naming a specific shot to be taken, can work wonders.

Decrease in Free Throw Opportunities

Too many 3-point attempts can lead to a decrease in free throw opportunities due to the lack of post scoring attempts and dribble penetration. This creates a wide range of problems including lack of scoring from the foul line, reduced opportunities to substitute following a made free throw and reduced opportunities to set the press by substituting following a made free throw.

The opponent does not experience foul trouble as a result of the lack of penetration or post feeds. This further exacerbates the situation when late in the game the opponent can foul to protect a lead due to the offense not being in the bonus. It eliminates the strategy of attacking the opponent's best offensive player with dribble penetration in an effort to force the player to foul and as a result get into early foul trouble.

Perimeter Lapses

The term perimeter lapse is used to describe when too many perimeter shots in a row have been taken with the result being no post touches or dribble penetration attempts. Perimeter lapses are the leading causes of scoring droughts, loss of free throw opportunities and stagnant offense. Requiring players to enter the ball into the post or drive the lane is the only way to break a perimeter lapse. Using a set play that only obtains a lay-up can be an effective way to break a perimeter lapse.

Stagnant Offense

Stagnant offense results when players take a 3-point shot too early in the offense too often. The effect of stagnant offense is players standing on offense eliminating purposeful offensive movement. The best cure for this is to use a pass restriction requiring a specified number of passes before a shot can be taken.

4

Twelve Necessary Components of a 3-Point Attack

Good 3-point shooting teams do not just happen. It requires an investment of time, energy and effort on the part of the coaches and the players. In order to create a program capable of producing solid 3-point shooting teams, twelve components must be integrated into the teaching, practice sessions and mental approach of the team each season, year after year. The twelve components are:

- System of teaching
- System of shooting
- System of shot selection
- System of evaluating players
- Disciplined players
- An inside game
- A penetration game
- Spacing on offense
- Passing
- An offensive system that sets up 3-point shots
- Teach the mid-range pull-up jump shot
- Patience as a coach

System of Teaching

Great coaches are great teachers. They plan everything in great detail and invest considerable time and effort into determining the best way to teach skills, concepts, offense and defense. A careful examination of the great coaches will show each of these coaches was systematic in their approach to teaching their sport.

This system of teaching is a carefully crafted plan integrating fundamentals, tactics and strategy into the most effective order of teaching. Each piece of the puzzle is added at just the right time in order to be the most effective. Players are able to learn quicker, be successful sooner and execute better when they are in such a structured, systematic learning environment.

What is the best system of teaching? Every coach has a different personality and as a result, there can be no single master teaching system. Additional factors to consider are the tempo and style of play being taught and the fundamentals required to execute these systems successfully.

System of Shooting

There are several universal principles involved in teaching shooting and shooting correctly. Beyond that, there are several sound methods or approaches to shooting that are effective and will produce excellent results. Just as there is no one best system of teaching, there is no one best system of teaching shooting.

Please do not misunderstand what I am saying. There are several methods of shooting that are heads and shoulders above the rest. Just be aware there is more than one way to skin the cat so to speak. Again, invest the time to research different systems and find the system that will work the best with your approach to teaching the game, the players in your program and the situation you find yourself coaching in.

What is important is a well thought out and consistent approach to shooting is used. The system must also include a sound teaching methodology that will integrate into the overall system of teaching used to implement the entire program system.

System of Shot Selection

Shot selection is one of the most difficult concepts to teach. It involves time, score, available shot opportunities, being squared up and open, offensive rebounding positioning and hardest of all to instill, an accurate assessment on the part of the player of his/her shooting abilities.

Constructing a systematic approach gives the players guidelines to follow when making decisions about shot selection. A simple approach is to require players to be squared up, balanced, open, within their shooting range and the time and score permits taking the shot.

System of Evaluating Players

The hardest part of teaching shot selection is getting players to understand the realistic limits of their shooting ability. I have found the best way to get this point across with out crushing a player, and an effective way to at least show parents the reason why their child has restrictions placed on their shooting opportunities, is to use a range test.

This approach takes a bit of time to administer but it has it advantages. In addition to players having physical evidence of the limitations of their shooting range, players are told they can always retest again in the future and if they improve their range, some of the restrictions on their shot selection will be lifted.

Disciplined Players

Coach Bobby Knight defined discipline as knowing what had to be done, how to do it, when to do it and doing it that way every time. So many factors go into good shot selection, developing the ability to shoot the 3-point shot and having the ability to resist the temptation to simply take a 3-point shot.

An Inside Game

The 3-point shot was instituted to open up defenses and give post players more space to operate. While the rule did have the effect it was intended to, good defensive coaches adapted by placing tremendous pressure on the perimeter players and 3-point shooters, taking away good 3-point shots.

The counter to this defensive tactic is to enter the ball into the offensive low post, forcing the defense to relent on the perimeter pressure in order to defend the inside game. Good 3-point shooting teams who do not have opportunities built into the offense for post play opportunities or do not have an effective offensive post player, will face a season where good opponents can afford to extend their defense with little fear of being hurt by inside scoring.

A Penetration Game

Penetration into the interior of the defense forces the defense to rotate, creating recovery situations that are difficult for the defense to successfully recover from.

In addition to creating open shot opportunities, other positives of a penetration game include lay-up opportunities and the ability to draw fouls on the opponent's defenders.

Spacing on Offense

Proper spacing is essential to every offense regardless of the style or system of play and the type of shot the offense is attempting to obtain. Good spacing forces the defense to use one defender to guard one offensive player if playing man-to-man defense or one area if playing a zone defense. Poor spacing allows one defender to cover two offensive players. It also restricts the ability of the offense to move freely, dribble penetrate, cut effectively, feed the post and set effective screens.

Passing

The most effective way, and the quickest, to move the ball is to pass the ball. Not only must players have the ability to pass the ball, they must pass with accuracy, away from the defense and have the ability to select the correct type of pass for the given situation.

An Offensive System That Sets Up 3-point Shots

Regardless of whether the offensive system is built around rule based offense such as motion offense, a continuity offense such as the flex or set plays such as quick hitters, if the system of play does not provide spacing and opportunities to create open 3-point shots as a normal part of offensive play, it will be difficult to successfully incorporate the 3-point shot into the offense.

The primary issue is one of spacing. The perimeter players must be space far enough apart to be behind the 3-point line and to create opportunities to feed the post or penetrate and create shooting opportunities. The offensive system utilized must also feature offensive building blocks that are appropriate for creating open 3-point shots.

Teach the Mid-Range Pull-up Jump Shot

In the age of the dunk and the three-point shot, the mid-range pull-up jump shot seems to be a lost art. Defenses are becoming more sophisticated in defending the fast break and the three point shot, often deliberately conceding the mid-range pull-up jump shot in order to defend both the lay-up and the three-point shot.

Teaching the pull-up jump shot provides attackers and point guards with a deadly weapon for their arsenal, prevents charging fouls on hard drives to the goal and further challenges the opponent's defense.

Patience as a coach

John Wooden has been quoted as saying "good things take time. And they should." He's right of course.

5

Universal Basic Principles of Shooting

Number 1

The Most Important Shooting Coach a Player Can Have is Him(Her)self

Player's benefit from instruction from coaches who are experts in teaching kills, particularly how to shoot a basketball. During a game, a player does not have the benefit of having a coach observe his or her shot repeatedly to find the flaws causing the player to consistently miss shots.

For this reason, the player must understand how to correct flaws in his or her own shot. Players must have enough technical knowledge about shooting combined with the knowledge of how their own shot "feels" kinesthetically when performed correctly. This allows the player to recognize what is wrong with their shot and correct it during a game.

Number 2

Hold a High One-Second Follow Through

There is more than one correct method to shot a basketball. Some methods are better than others. Even if two players are taught to shoot with the "best" method, there will be slight differences in the mechanics of their shots.

Regardless of the method of shooting the great shooters all hold a high, one-second in duration, follow through after shooting the ball. A high follow through can be described as when the player's shooting elbow is above the eyebrow following the release of the shot. The shooter holds this position, or

13

pose, for a long one-second count with the proper follow through. The last finger to leave the ball must be in line with the shooter's target.

The high follow through will ensure the shot will be close to the desired 60-degree arc while in flight. The follow through ensure the ball will have the desired back spin which increases the likelihood the shot will go in if it should impact the rim.

Number 3

Get the Ball Up – 60-Degree Arc

The arc of the ball during its flight to the goal is important. If the arc is "too flat," or too low a degree of arc, the effect is to reduce the area available for the ball to pass through the rim. Flat shots also result in hard, long rebounds.

If the arc is "too high," called by some a "moon ball," the ball may have the entire area of the goal to pass through, but if the flight path of the ball is slightly off, the impact will be so hard there will be no chance for shooter's roll to cause the ball to go in. The result will be a high, hard and long rebound.

The optimal arc for a shot is a 60-degree arc. It is "flat" enough it won't take a high, hard long rebound if the flight path of the shot is slightly off, giving the shot a chance for shooter's roll to work. The arc is "high" enough to make the maximum area of the goal available for the ball to pass through.

Number 4

Always be Moving Toward the Basket

Moving away from the basket or drifting to the left or right while shooting will introduce errors into either the shooting mechanics of the shot or the flight path of the ball.

It is essential the ball travel in a straight line towards the goal. To ensure this, the shooter should always be "moving toward the basket" in a straight line. This is not to imply the shooter should lunge or run at the basket. Instead the shooter should be moving in a straight line towards the basket prior to the shot. This way all the energy or drift in the shot that is not desirable moves in a straight line. The flight path of the shot will remain straight.

If a shot must be missed, it is desirable to miss long or short (**Number 10**) and not left or right. This will allow the shot some chance to still go in with shooter's roll.

Number 5

Shoot on the Way Up

The ball should be released in the shooting motion just prior to the top of the shooter's jump, in the case of a jump shot, or the upward motion in the case of a set shot.

Releasing the ball too early will cause the shot to be short and often players will compensate by "throwing the ball." Releasing the ball after the peek of the release will also cause problems. The shot will fall short and players compensate by throwing the ball. Both result in erratic shooting.

Releasing just before the peek of the shot or the shooting motion allows for the smoothest transfer of energy and the greatest amount of control and accuracy in the shot.

Number 6

Sight a Specific Target When Shooting - The More Specific the Better

The human brain is in many ways like a targeting computer in an ICBM. The more specific the information the targeting computer receives, the more accurate the missile strike will be. The more specific a target a shooter has, the more accurately the brain will target the shot.

Players who have excellent mechanics but are poor shooters, when asked what they aim at or what target they sight, often respond they look at the entire goal. Great shooters have a very specific target. It could be the one-inch of rim opposite from where the shooter is shooting or it could be two inches above the dead center of the rim. Regardless of the target, the key is the shooter must have a very specific target.

A note about targets, shooters who use the area just behind the front of the rim as their target miss a high percentage of shots by shooting short. The brain has the ball travel exactly where the shooter aimed but most shots fall just a little short, thus the shooters who use this area as their target tend to shoot short.

Number 7

Backspin is What Allows Misses to Go In

Have a player take a basketball and toss it with no backspin so that it bounces on the court. When the ball impacts on the court it will develop slight front spin, causing the ball to move in the direction opposite from the player who tossed the ball.

Now have a player take a basketball and toss it with backspin on the ball. Now when the ball impacts the court, the backspin stops and the ball bounces straight up with no spin on the ball at all, falling just an inch or two behind where the initial contact point was. This phenomenon is what creates "shooter's roll."

A shot with no backspin or with front spin will not go through the rim when the shot is off just enough for the ball to impact the top of the rim, creating a miss. A ball with backspin that impacts the top of the rim will bounce straight up, remaining in the area over the rim, allowing some chance that the ball will pass through the rim when it descends.

Number 8

A Shooter Should Land Just Slightly Forward of His/Her Own Footprints

Shooters do not want to drift when shooting a shot. Drifting to the left, right, front or to the rear decreases the shooter's accuracy and increases the potential for mechanical errors to creep into the shot. For example, drifting to the right on a jump shot by a right handed jump shooter will tend to cause the shooter to turn his body into the shot towards the left, pushing the shot line of the ball to the left, causing the shot to be missed to the left.

A good tool for shooters to use to prevent drifting is the two-inch rule in which the shooter lowers his rear two inches lower in the triple threat when stopping and then raising up the two inches again. This simple skill directs all of the directional momentum, which can cause a shooter to drift in one direction or another, downward, eliminating it as a problem.

Another good tool for shooters to use to prevent drifting is the idea of landing in their own footprints, with permission to land just slightly forward if necessary. A shooter does want to land just slightly the forward, the slight forward momentum of the shooter's body helps to both propel the ball forward to the goal and to align the shot with the goal.

By attempting to land in their own footprints, players will naturally land just slightly forward but still in alignment with their original take off point. Telling players they have permission to land just slightly forward of their footprints prevents the player from overcorrecting and in doing so, causing technique problems.

Number 9

Basketball Players Must Warm-up Their Shot

Shooters, like a pitcher in baseball warming up his arm before pitching, must warm up their shots. Too many players walk into a gym, pick up a basketball and shooting three point shots immediately. The good and great shooters always warm up their shot.

To properly warm-up a shot, a player needs a set routine that emphasizes muscle memory and correct technique. Another essential element of warming up a shot is for the player to start shooting for makes two feet from the goal and then slowly working out to the player's maximum shooting range. When players use this type of an approach to warming up their shot, they are much more consistent and their field goal percentage is higher.

The key element of this type of approach is the process of starting in close for the first shots and then working out to the edge of the shooter's range. This concept is key because the player has immediate success in terms of making shots. There is nothing that boosts a shooter's confidence like seeing the ball go through the rim and swishing the net!

Number 10

If You Miss a Shot, Miss Long or Short, Not Left or Right

If a player misses a shot, it should be long or short and not left and right. Players should always strive to keep their shot line straight. This is an easy repair to make to a shot. The player can simply follow through with a little less force to shorten the shot or a little more force for to lengthen the shot.

Shots that are missed to the left or right can have a myriad of issues in the shooting technique such as the player was not squared up properly, pushed the ball with the balance hand, etc, are more difficult technique issues to address.

The primary reason a player wants to make certain he misses long or short but not left or right is "shooter's roll." A shot that is too long or too short but has the correct amount of backspin and is at a 60-degree arc will bounce more or less straight up in the area over the rim. A good percentage of these "misses" will go in. Shots missed to the left or right will bounce away from the goal after impact. Long or short is easy to fix. Left or right is much more difficult a flaw to repair.

Number 11

Use a "Shot Line"

The concept of a shot line is critical in "aiming a shot" and in players having the ability to self-correct a missed shot. The shot line is the straight line between the exact target the player is shooting at and the last finger of the high, one-second follow through that touched the ball when released.

In addition, depending on the method of shooting the player has been taught, the shot line must include the correct alignment of key body parts upon completion of the shot. For example, a player who has been taught to start the shot with a shooting pocket on the side of their body of their dominant hand will have a shot line of big toe, knee, elbow and index finger when holding a high, one-second follow through. The balance hand must be examined as well as it can impact the shot line as well.

If the shot line has been executed properly, the flight path of the ball will be straight and in line with the desired target.

6

General Concepts for 3-Point Shooting

Number 12

The Poorest Shot in the Game of Basketball

The poorest shot in the game of basketball is when a player stands with one foot, or part of a foot, on the 3-point line when shooting. This shot is only worth two points if it is made yet it is the poorest percentage 2-point shot that can be taken. Simply moving back far enough to make certain both feet are behind the 3-point line makes the shot a good one.

The value of the made attempt is three points instead of two. The percentages of shooting come into play in this example. A good field goal percentage for a 2-point shooter is 45-50%. A good field goal percentage for a 3-point shooter is 33%. If a shooter takes 100 2-point field goal attempts and makes fifty percent of the attempts, the shooter will score 100 points. If the same shooter takes 100 3-point shots and makes thirty-three percent of the attempts, the shooter will score 99 points.

A 2-point shot attempt that a shooter is going to make on average only thirty-three percent of the time is a poor shot. A 3-point shot rewards the shooter with an extra point when the shot is made even though the field goal percentage for a shot taken from roughly the same distance is still only thirty-three percent.

If a player is going to take a thirty-three percent shot, it needs to be worth three points when the player makes it. If not, over the course of the game or a season, the additional missed shots will haunt that player's team because when the shot is made, the reward is only two points.

Number 13

Know Where the 3-Point Line is Without Looking

Players must develop a keen sense of awareness concerning the location of the 3-point line. The time it takes to look down to make certain the player is behind the line is the time it will take for an aggressive, hustling defender to closeout with high hands on the shooter.

Players who feel uncertain about the location of the 3-point line will shoot the ball with less confidence, reducing the likelihood of making the shot. When trailing by three points with little time remaining in the game, it is particularly critical a player know where the line is without looking. No player wants to make the game tying 3-point shot only to discover the field goal was only worth two points due to the player being inside or standing on the 3-point line.

Number 14

Know Your Best Shooting Area/Spot and Work to Get Shots in That Area

In a perfect world, every good shooter would be able to shoot equally effectively from any location on the court. The truth is shooters have areas or spots on the court where that shooter is much more effective.

Both coaches and the shooter must be aware of this fact and work to obtain as many shots as possible from this location of the court. It does not make sense to force a shooter to operate in less than optimal shooting conditions in a game.

Shooters must work to improve their proficiency from any location for shots located in 3-point range. Coaches must devise ways to obtain as many shots from their 3-point shooter's best shooting areas.

Practice is the time to work to improve and increase skills. During a game the object is to perform at maximum efficiency to give the team every possible chance to win the game. Both shooter and coach have a responsibility to the team to make sure the 3-point shooter has the best opportunities available to score 3-point goals.

Number 15

Know the Time and Score

Does the team need a 3-pt. goal to tie or possession of the ball to run out the clock? How much time is left? These are factors the coach, point guard and players must know as the game draws to a conclusion. Please note, every player must understand "time and score" rules. Many games have been lost because teams passed up easy 2-point field goals that would have tied the game to force up a desperation 3-point field goal.

Time and score situations must be reviewed regularly in practice. Coaches must have a well-structured plan for dealing with end of game scenarios, including how players are to obtain specific shots at a specific time, be the shot a 2-point field goal or a 3-point field goal.

Number 16

Missed 3-Point Shots Take Longer Rebounds

Offensive rebounds are important for any team. Offensive rebounds are even more important for a team who takes a large number of 3-point shots during the course of the game. One of the advantages of this approach for a team who is smaller in stature is the longer rebound of a missed 3-point attempt. Most rebounds will travel one-third of the distance from which the shot was taken before hitting the court. This extra distance allows smaller players to use speed, hustle and savvy to obtain more rebounds.

Increased fouls on the opponent, more shooting opportunities and often a higher field goal percentage are all positive outcomes derived from offensive rebounds.

Number 17

Think in Terms of a Set Shot

Players tend to think in terms of taking a jump shot when deciding to shoot. While 3-point shooter can and do successfully take jump shots, it is wiser to think more in terms of a set shot.

The guiding principle is one of control. The less movement in the shot, the easier it is to control the shot. Which is an easier shot in the game of golf, a put six inches away from the hole or chipping the ball in from 45 feet away? The put has a very short backswing and a short distance for the ball to travel. The chip shot requires a longer swing and has a much greater distance to travel. The put is the easier shot because of the shorter distance and the reduced amount of body movement required to make the shot.

The same is true with a 3-point shot attempt. The distance is greater, making the shot more difficult. Any thing that can be done to reduce the amount of movement will increase the chances of the shot attempt being successful.

Number 18

If Necessary, Lower the Shooting Pocket

For weaker players and some girls, in order to obtain the thrust necessary to have the range to shoot from 3-point distance, it may be necessary to lower the shooting pocket prior to shooting the ball.

Number 19

Shoot as High as the Top of the Blackboard

What does a 60-degree arc look like? Abstract ideas are great for coaches but players often need visual cues to measure their performance. An easy visual cue for players to use to determine if they are shooting with proper arc on their 3-point shots while practicing or in games is for the ball at the peak of its flight to be roughly level with the top of the backboard.

If the ball is below the top of the backboard, the arc is too low. If the ball is above top of the backboard, the arc of the ball is too high.

7

Principles of Shooting off the Dribble

Number 20

Move Towards the Goal

Negative motion for a shooter can be defined as any force moving in the direction away from the goal. Fade away shots, shots in which the shooter falls or fades away in a direction away from the goal is one such example and results in a low percentage of shot attempts being successfully converted.

When shooting 3-point shots off the dribble, it is preferable for the shooter to be moving in the direction of the goal. An excellent example of this is a point guard pulling up on the fast break for a 3-point shot attempt. Another example is a 3-point shooter who has received an inside/out pass from a post player fanning the ball out taking a dribble to move into range if the pass was received too far out for the 3-point shooter to be effective.

Dribbling away from the goal increases the difficulty involved in stopping any momentum the shooter has created moving in a direction away from the goal. For example, if the shooter has executed a dribble off from the baseline and the defense has reacted by collapsing on the post or moving to cover the now open 3-point shooter who has filled in on the baseline, leaving the shooter in possession of the ball open for a 3-point attempt.

The momentum created by executing the dribble off is moving away from the goal. The shooter must make certain all negative motion away from the goal has been eliminated when the shooter squared up on the inside foot. Failure to do so will often result in the shooter pushing the ball to the left or right in an effort to compensate for the drift caused by negative motion.

This issue can certainly be overcome with drills designed to practice eliminating the negative motion. It is always desirable and preferable, when possible, to be driving towards the goal and not dribbling away from the goal when shooting a 3-point shot attempt.

Number 21

Should Not Be Closely Guarded

Driving into the lane to shoot a jump shot or a power shot is a skill requiring the ability to shoot while closely guarded. Because the margin of error in the shot is dramatically reduced due to the shooter's proximity to the goal, a closely guarded shot in the paint, particularly by a post player, is a good shot and for a skilled player.

The increase in distance from the goal for a 3-point shot magnifies the impact of any error in shooting motion and the shot line, increasing the likelihood of a missed shot. For this reason, it is essential any added difficulty in the shot be eliminated for 3-point shot attempts. In this instance, 3-point shot attempts off the dribble should not be closely guarded.

Number 22

Step Plant for Shooting off the Dribble

Players may stop by executing a jump stop or a step plant. Both methods are fine and players must master both stopping techniques. Post players are well served with this method of stopping prior to a shot due to the likelihood of contact and the need for a quick stop prior to the shot attempt. The same is true for perimeter players who have ventured into the lane area with dribble penetration.

While slightly slower, the benefits of using the step plant for many 3-point shooters are significant. The increased sense of rhythm in the act of shooting increases the confidence level of the shooter along with making the shooting motion smoother.

The footwork involved with the step plan technique also makes squaring up off the dribble much easier and helps the shooter to eliminate unwanted negative motion away from the goal prior to taking the shot.

Number 23

Last Dribble Must be a Hard One

When attacking the goal, regardless of the player's distance from the goal, it is essential the ball be placed in the shooting pocket as quickly as possible as the player faces up to the basket, to either pass to a teammate or to take an open shot.

To bring the ball as quickly as possible to the shooting pocket, the last dribble taken should be a hard dribble, increasing the velocity of the ball as it is brought to the shooting pocket. A soft last dribble often results in the ball being located in areas other than the shooting pocket, resulting in a fatally flawed shot even before the shooter releases the ball for the shot attempt.

8

Principles of Shooting off the Pass

Number 24

Set the Shot Up Before Catching the Pass

Being quick but not in a hurry sounds like a strange concept (**Number 49**). The best method for achieving this for a 3-point shooter who is not in possession of the ball is to be ready to shoot prior to the arrival of the ball via a pass.

This requires the shooter to be squared up or in the process of squaring up, the knees bent and the hands in the appropriate location to receive the pass. By completing all of the preparation to shoot prior to catching the ball, the shooter is able to speed up the shoot (be quick) without having to rush the shot (hurrying).

Number 25

Bring the Ball to the Shooting Pocket First

The use of the shot line as a means to insure an accurate flight path to the target is essential. For the shot line to be effective and accurate, the ball must be in the correct position prior to the start of the shot.

When shooters catch passes the ball can be in a variety of locations, most of which are not the shooting pocket. A miss-aligned shot line, meaning the ball is to the left or the right of the straight line to the intended target, will result in a mechanically incorrect shot, nearly always resulting in a missed 3-point shot attempt.

Shooters must develop the habit of always bringing the ball into the shooting pocket after catching a pass and making certain the ball is in proper alignment in relationship to the shot line. If the pass was off target, a two-inch shot fake often will help the shooter bring the ball into correct alignment and return the ball to the correct position in the shooting pocket prior to the start of the shot.

Number 26

Step Directly Into an Inside/Out Pass

When the 3-point shooter's defender has collapsed to help on the post or the shooter has stepped into a seam, the post play is able to fan the ball out for an open 3-point attempt. One of the most desirable of all passes to shoot a 3-point shot, the shooter should catch the ball with one foot a step ahead of the other, shortening the pass. The knees should be bent and the shooter squared up to the goal, allowing the back foot to be brought forward upon the arrival and reception of the ball. This technique provides both rhythm to the shot and forces the shooter to prepare to shoot in advance of the arrival of the ball.

Number 27

Use Hand Targets to Communicate

Passing requires communication between the player in possession of the ball and the player who desires to receive the ball. Verbal communication can be misunderstood or not heard during the chaos of a game. Visual signals with hands cannot be misunderstood and for this reason is a more effective method of communicating a cutter's intent to the passer.

Three basic hand signals must be learned by all players, allowing the cutter/shooter to communicate intent and the passer to anticipate where to pass the ball away from the defense. The first is an extended open hand, indicating the direction away from the goal the cutter/shooter intends to cut towards.

The second hand signal is the clinched fist, indicating the shooter/cutter intends to cut "backdoor," in the direction of the goal. This cut is used when the defense is applying intense overplay denial defense, a common tactic used against excellent 3-point shooters in the desire to prevent the shooter from receiving the ball beyond the 3-point line.

The third and final hand signal is used to indicate the shooter is open and ready to shoot upon receiving the ball. This signal is indicated by the shooter having hands in the shooting pocket, knees bent ready to shoot and being squared up to the goal. The shooter needs only to catch the pass in order to shoot if the passer makes an accurate pass directly into the shooting pocket.

Top: Directional hand target.
Right: Backdoor hand target.
Lower: Ready to shoot hand target.
Photographs by Maddy Copello.

Number 28

Concept of Face-up/Square up

Players are told constantly by their coaches to "square up" before shooting. While seemingly a simple concept, players struggle at times with this concept because of its "relative nature." Being correctly squared up on one spot of the court does not mean the player is squared up when facing the same direction but in a different location on the court.

Being squared up means the player is "square" to the basket. The toes of the shooter's feet are pointing directly at either side of the rim. The shooter's shoulders are square to the basket and most important, the shooter's shot line is lined up correctly with the goal.

Players must develop the habit of "facing-up" every time a pass is caught. Facing up, being square to the basket, allows the player to look under the net and immediately determine if a teammate is open or a shot is available.

Not Squared Up

Squared Up

9

Essential Basic Skills

Number 29

Fundamentals Are Key!

A team filled with great 3-point shooters will not be able to take advantage of its shooting skill unless those players can all run, cut, stop, start, turn (pivot), v-cut, pass, catch, dribble and defend. And those are only a few of the essential basic skills all basketball players must master.

John Wooden believed fundamentals were so important he practiced the basics of footwork during the one hour allotted for practice at the game site of the NCAA National Championship game. With 10 NCAA National Championships to his credit, this is a fact worth taking note of.

Number 30

Free Throws and Lay-ups Win Games

This is a book about fine-tuning the 3-point segment of your team offense. As a coach I long ago embraced the 3-point shot and love what the shot can do for a team and how the 3-point shot is an equalizer. But it is an unquestionable fact that lay-ups and free throws are still how you win games.

Turnovers lead to fast break lay-ups that are "easy" scoring opportunities. The penetration game must end with a successful lay-up on a consistent basis in order to create the passing opportunities for a score that occur when the defense is forced to rotate to help on the penetration.

Teams who are unable to score on their easy scoring opportunities will struggle to score against solid defensive teams. The penetrator who cannot make a lay-up will neither score nor force the defense to rotate, creating opportunities to pass for a score, draw a foul or both.

Number 31

Free Throws Matter!

It is the same shot from the same spot and with no defender. It is literally a free shot awarded to the shooter for being fouled or for a technical infraction by the opponent.

With most basketball games being decided by six points or less, free throws are critical for success. Games are often decided in the final moments by free throws. The team that consistently shoots well from the foul line has an excellent chance of winning. Players who shoot over 70% from the foul line are valuable assets who are likely to earn playing time during the critical stages of a game.

Free throws, and lay-ups, are not glamorous but these two fundamental skills are essential for both success for both the team and the individual player.

TEAMs who emphasize the fast break and the 3-point shot generate a large number of opportunities for lay-ups, and in doing so draw a large number of free throw attempts. Failure to convert on both the lay-up opportunities and free throws resulting from fouls is the same as turning the ball over.

Photograph by Dave Shutts

Number 32

Lay-ups, Lay-ups, Lay-ups

Photograph by Dave Shutts

The dunk is exciting! The three-point shot has been good for the game, opening up the inside for post play and the penetration game. Pressing defenses and pressure man-to-man defense create chaos and turnovers. Passing can be a thing of beauty when executed by a gifted passer.

As important as all of the above are, after the TEAM concept, the two most important things in the game of basketball are free throws and lay-ups. It is that simple.

The fast break generates large numbers of lay-up opportunities that in turn result in numerous free throw opportunities. Failure to convert lay-ups allows the opponent to extend its defense, pressure the ball more aggressiveness, cover three-point shooters and not have to fear giving up easy scoring opportunities.

It cannot be stressed enough, free throws and lay-ups win basketball games. TEAMs who fail to consistently take advantage of these high percentage scoring opportunities will lose a large percentage of their games. Coaches must place a heavy emphasis on the importance of these two skills.

Number 33

Place a Heavy Emphasis on Fundamentals!

Remember the rule *"players do what their coach emphasizes, not what their coach teaches!"* Paying lip service to fundamentals by talking about the importance of these skills and not following up with daily repetitions combined with insistence of the use of fundamentals during games teaches players fundamentals are not really that important.

Whose fault is it when the game tying 3-point shot is negated because the shooter traveled if there has been no daily work on the proper execution of pivoting, passing and catching and proper footwork to set-up a shot?

The best offense in the world will be quickly negated if the players do not possess the basic, essential fundamental skills of the game of basketball to execute the offense. Emphasize the importance of mastery of these skills! Do it through repeated exposures to the skills and the concept of mastery of fundamentals on a daily basis and through as many different means as possible.

Players will recognize through the constant repetition and the constant use of various means to communicate this key life principle that fundamentals are important. The emphasis through this approach is what will truly teach the players this concept.

Footwork

Number 34

Starts, Stops and Turns

Outstanding defense that forces a turnover is one thing. Committing a turnover due to traveling is another. There is no acceptable reason for traveling. Mastering the essential fundamentals of start steps, jump and stride stops and turning (pivoting) not only eliminate turnovers, they are essential components of a penetration game. For 3-point shooters, the penetration game is an essential complimentary game to relieve defensive pressure.

Number 35

Stopping Matters Too

The ability to stop is as important as the ability to initiate movement. For shooters, the ability to stop with excellent balance and no extra motion, forward or to the sides, is essential.

Whether stopping off the dribble, filling a lane on the fast break or cutting off a screen, great shooters are ready to stop with balance, catch the ball, face-up in triple threat and shoot the ball in a smooth, fluid and controlled motion.

Basketball players have two methods of stopping quickly, the jump stop and the stride, or one-two stop using a step-plant. The jump stop is executed by taking a final long, low step, jumping in the air a few inches off the ground and landing on both feet at the same time with the knees bent, back straight, chin level and head centered. The advantage of the jump stop is the player can pivot on either foot if in possession of the ball.

The stride stop, or step-plant method, is often easier for female players and is appropriate for any player when already faced up to the goal and stepping into the pass for a shot or picking up the dribble for a shot.

The skill is executed by stepping on the inside (towards the middle of the court) foot first using a heel-toe plant followed by planting the outside foot. After planting the inside foot first, if necessary the shooter must face-up before putting the plant foot down. The knees must be bent, back straight, chin level and head centered.

Passing

Number 36

Use the Pass to Key the Shot

The location of the pass can help the shooter determine where the shot will be located. This is particularly true for post players. Passing the ball to the high side, the side away from the baseline, lets the post player know to turn to the middle for the shot. A baseline side bounce pass lets the post player know the shot is towards the baseline. A pass directly into the post player's chest indicates the defender is directly behind and the post player will have to beat the defender with fakes and a post move.

Just as the pass can key the location of the shot for a post player, it can communicate shot location to a 3-point shooter. A pass directly into the shooting pocket lets the 3-point shooter know it is a catch and shoot opportunity. Passing the ball to the left or right of the shooter can move the shooter in the direction of the open shot, or if necessary, silently inform the shooter there is no 3-point shot available.

In the case of a struggling 3-point shooter, a smart point guard may choose to limit shooting opportunities for the shooter by making passes capable of being caught without danger of a turnover, but not in a location where the struggling shooter is able to take a shot. A pass that moves the struggling shooter often will give the defense plenty of time to recover and closeout, preventing a shot but not movement of the ball on offense.

Number 37

Throw Frozen Ropes

There is never an excuse for a bad pass, in a game, practice or simply picking up the balls after practice. Emphasize this concept by insisting every pass made is a "frozen rope." Picture taking a piece of string, soaking it in water and then stretching it out in a freezer, when the water soaked string has frozen and is removed from the freezer, it will stay perfectly straight and flat. All passes should have this same flat and straight aspect (with the exception of "drop passes" on the fast break). The only way to achieve this is to pass the ball with energy, or zip, ensuring the ball will arrive at its target quickly.

Number 38

Pass Away From the Defense

Turnovers due to intercepted passes are usually a result of passing the ball to a teammate. Sounds silly, but it is true. Unless the teammate is wide open for a shot, the ball should never be passed directly to the teammate. Instead, the ball must be passed away from the defense. This includes both the defender guarding the passer (**Photograph 38-A**) and the cutter (**Photograph 38-B**).

Photograph 38-A by Maddy Copello

Photograph 38-B by Maddy Copello

Number 39

Shorten the pass

Not only must the passer pass the ball away from the defense using a frozen rope, the cutter/shooter must "shorten the pass" by stepping in the direction of the oncoming pass to meet the ball. This decreases the chances of the defense intercepting the pass and increases the likelihood of a foul on an aggressive denial defender.

This technique also allows a shooter who is coming off a screen or who has simply made a flash cut to set up his/her footwork to catch the ball, face-up, get on balance and in a smooth continuous motion shoot the ball.

Players must be trained to create this habit. The technique utilizes a start step, the same start step a player uses to pass a ball, execute a direct drive or crossover step or to jump stop. The player steps towards the ball with an aggressive, long, low start step, propelling the player towards the ball.

10

Shot Selection Rules for the 3-Point Shot

For Players:

Number 40

Always Obey Rules for Time and Score

There are times when possession of the ball is more valuable than scoring more points. There are other times when any open shot that can be taken quickly (but not in a hurry) is a good shot. In other words, the time and the score in a game can dictate what is and what is not a good shot. The guidelines for how time and score determine what is a good or bad shot will vary from team to team. Regardless, shooters must always be aware of the time and score and take these factors into their decision making process when determining if a shot is a good shot or not.

Number 41

Only Shoot 3s If You Have Been Green-lighted

If a player has not been green-lighted to take 3-point shots, that player must never take a 3-point shot in a game unless there is no other option available and time is about to run out. Any violation of this rule should result in an immediate consultation with the master motivator, Mr. Bench. Players are often a poor judge of their actual ability and the coaching staff must be responsible for establishing guidelines for who is permitted to take what type of shots, establishing shot selection rules and determining a fair and valid method of evaluating shoot ability. Administering a range test to each member of the team goes a long way to establishing in the minds of both the players and the coaches who does and does not have the ability to shoot from any given range.

Players may disagree with being limited in their choices for shot selection but are much more willing to play within the guidelines set forth when the coach has a measurable and demonstrable means of evaluating who is green-lighted for shooting the 3-point shot and who is not.

Range tests also serve as a valuable motivational tool. Players should be allowed to re-test on a regular basis and if the player passes the test, receive the desired green-light to shoot the 3-point shot. The range test provides players with a clear idea of how much the player must improve, from where and can provide self-feedback during individual shooting practice.

Improvement is the name of the game and anything that helps players understand the game, their skill level and how to improve is a valuable tool for coaches.

Number 42

Be Squared Up

Watch the great shooters. They all square up before they shoot. Being square to the goal is critical in order to have a shot line that is accurate. Keep in mind if the shooter is going to miss the shot, the miss must be long or short and not to the left or right. Not being squared up will produce a shot line that is off to the left or right, preventing shooter's roll from helping the ball go in after the initial miss.

Number 43

Be on Balance

This is a good principle to obey regardless of the shot taken. An off balance shot has little chance of going in. Balance is essential in order for a shooter to be able to execute in proper sequence and timing the proper mechanics of a shot.

Number 44

Be Open

Being open for a shot will vary from player to player. Some players will need more time and space for a shot to be an open shot. Other players will need very little space and time for a shot to be open. What is an open shot can vary by position as well. Post players would love to have a space of five or six feet between the post player and the nearest defensive player. Post players nearly always shoot with physical contact and a defender in close proximity. The same is not true for 3-point shooters who require more space and time for a shot to be open. Regardless of the type of shot, players must have a thorough understanding of what an "open shot" is for every member of their team.

Number 45

Does a Teammate Have a Better Shot?

The best shooter available must take the best available shot. Does a teammate have a better shot? If the answer is yes, then that teammate should take the shot. Or so it would seem.

Time and score once again raises its head. Sometimes the time and the score dictates a less than desirable shot is the best shot to take. It is also essential for players to understand what is a good shot for one player is not necessarily a good shot for another player.

A reasonably open 3-point shot might be a better shot in some circumstances than an open twelve foot 2-point shot due to the ability of the player taking the shot. All of these variables are part of the equation in the shot selection process and player must be taught to recognize these variables, use judgment and discern who has the best shot.

Number 46

It Bears Saying – Be Beyond the 3-Point Line

The worse shot in the game of basketball is a 2-point shot where the shooter is standing on the 3-point shot line (See Concepts **Number 12** and **Number 13**). Players must develop a keen sense of court awareness. If a 3-point shot is needed then any shot worth less is unacceptable. Players must know without thinking they are taking the "right" shot.

Number 47

A Good Shot is a Good Shot – Even When it Does Not Go In!

Too many players, fans and even coaches view a missed shot as a bad shot. Still others believe any shot that goes in is a good shot. Nothing could be further from the truth and players need to be discouraged from adopting this idea as part of their decision making process for shot selection. Good shots are good shots, even when a good shot does not go in. A bad shot is still a bad shot, even if the ball finds a way to go through the rim.

Number 48

When Struggling, Make a Lay-up

Confidence is important for shooters. It can be a fragile commodity when the ball consistently won't fall and the shooter "feels" like he/she is shooting correctly in terms of mechanics and is following the rules of shot selection. There is nothing like watching the ball go through the rim to give a shooter's confidence a little boost. When a 3-point shooter is struggling, he/she should shoot a lay-up or the coach should run a set play to obtain the struggling shooter an easy lay-up. For a struggling shooter, a lay-up always makes the rim look bigger for the next shot.

Number 49

Be Quick but Not in a Hurry – or Don't Shoot!

Anything done in a hurry is usually not done well and that includes properly executing the mechanics of shooting a basketball. Rushing a shot causes a player to incorrectly time the various sequences of the shooting motion, creating errors in the shot.

Number 50

Be Aware of Rebounding Position

Is there a teammate in reasonable position to obtain an offensive rebound? For many teams, offensive rebounding is a major component of the overall offensive strategy. Teams who take a large number of 3-point shots often desire to obtain thirty-three present of all missed offensive shots. Other teams are not as concerned with obtaining a large number of offensive rebounds. If offensive rebounding is a major factor in the team's overall offensive strategy, shooters need to be taught to check the potential for a teammate being in position to obtain an offensive rebound.

Number 51

When in Doubt – Don't!

If a player has any doubt about whether or not to take a shot, the rule of thumb must always be don't! Hesitation, uncertainty or doubt will cause the player to make some type of mistake in the mechanics of shooting. It is always preferable to have possession of the ball than to force a bad shot and allow the opponent to obtain possession. If time permits, a good shot will become available with a little patience and offensive execution.

For Coaches:

Number 52

Once you Green-light a Player...

This one will be the hardest shot selection rule for coaches to follow. Once a player has passed the requirements to be green-lighted to shoot the 3-point shot, so long as the player follows the rules for shot selection that have been set forth, a coach needs to sit and hold his/her tongue. Undue criticism over some missed shots can damage a shooter's confidence. Players need to know their coach has an unwavering belief in the player's ability to shoot the ball well. Silence in the presence of several missed shots can say a lot, in a positive way, for a shooter. I am not saying let the ship go down to protect a shooter's confidence, simply use good judgment and remain silent as long as the shooter's struggles are within reason.

Number 53

Help a Struggling Shooter Get Back on Track

When a shooter is struggling, the coach must help the player obtain an easy shot. Lay-ups always make the rim look bigger (Concept **Number 47**) and can help a shooter shake whatever is mentally bothering the player. Running quick-hitters, placing restrictions on the offense and having the offense work to get the 3-point shooter shots from his/her favorite spots are all tools a coach can use to help a shooter get back on track.

Do not overlook bad shots by a struggling shooter. Emphasize the need to focus on good shot selection. There is a reason why good shots are labeled as such. These shots have a greater chance of going in. Reinforce the shot selection rules and encourage a struggling shooter to focus on the shot selection rules as well.

Number 54

Teach Shot Selection Rules – Then Let Your Players Go

Invest time effort and energy in teaching shot selection. Teach players how to shoot, how to get good shots and how to coach themselves when their shot needs a quick game time repair. Invest the time to teach players to understand the strategy and tactics involved in getting good shots, particularly good 3-point shots, and then turn your players loose.

When players are looking over their shoulders all game long to judge the reaction of their coach, they will never be able to play with the looseness and confidence necessary to truly play in the moment and feel the joy of the game.

Teams who play in the moment, the flow of the game and feel the joy of their sport are teams who execute with confidence, embrace the challenge of the adversity the game will bring and come the closest to playing to their potential game after game.

Number 55

Emphasize Time And Score

Players do what coaches emphasize, not what coaches teach. Shot selection is one of the most difficult concepts to teach due to all the variables involved. The most critical time for quality shot selection evolves around shots involving time and score as part of the decision making process.

Coaches must emphasize this concept and provide examples every day in practice and in as wide a range of scenarios as possible. Look for teachable moment on a daily basis in regard to the impact of time and score on shot selection for 3-point shooters.

Players need to understand variables such as time and points needed. If the game is winding down in its final seconds and the trailing team is behind by 3-points, only a 3-point shot is acceptable. If time is available and more than one score is required, a high percentage 2-point shot that can be quickly and easily obtained is a better shot than a quick, defended 3-point shot.

11

Strategy and the 3-Point Shot

Number 56

Strategy versus Tactics

Strategy is an overall approach to playing the game. Tactics are specific methods of obtaining a 3-point shot. For example, some teams want to play very fast, constantly attack and generate as many 3-point attempts as possible as quickly as possible. Teams who use this strategic approach to the game often prefer penetration tactics to generate 3-point shots.

Other teams want to play a controlled pace and will use screening tactics to obtain 3-point shots. These teams desire to produce fatigue through forcing the opponent to fight through screens and play defense for extended periods of time.

Number 57

Time and Score

There is a time to take 3-point shots and there is a time not to. Spend some time with a pad of paper, pen or pencil and create time and score scenarios. Determine the number of 2-point shots, 3-point shots and the combination of the two types of shots required to come from behind. Think about how your current team can best generate shots quickly to work at cutting into the lead.

Be aware that often 2-point shots can be obtained quicker and with greater ease than a 3-point shot late in a game. In addition, the 2-point shots will often result in a much higher conversion percentage. When the opponent holds a multiple possession lead, teams must recognize the fact 3-point shots are great but 2-point shots might be better.

As time winds down, 3-point shots might become necessary. Finally, if trailing by 3-points in the waning seconds, players must be aware a 3-point shot is required in order to tie the score.

It is not enough for players to be aware of time and score. Players must know how shots will be obtained quickly, who should take the shots and where the shots should be taken from. Rebounding schemes must be taken into consideration and decisions made about shooting a 2-point shot after an offensive rebound or should it be fanned out for a 3-point shot. All of this must be practiced on a regular basis.

Number 58

Playing Fast

Lay-ups and free throws are how you win games. Playing fast will generate lay-ups and free throw opportunities. It will also generate a large number of excellent 3-point shot opportunities. Adopting a fast breaking style of play is a bit of an all or nothing proposition. Lots of teams say they fast break, but when push comes to shove, these teams will set up and run half court offense.

This failure to commit to the all out running game ultimately means the team will be mediocre at both approaches to offense, half court and fast break. Make a strategic decision to commit to playing fast and all that is entailed with this approach to the game. It will mean changing how you conduct practice, look at the 3-point shot and play defense.

Number 59

Playing Deliberately

Playing slow, or at a deliberate pace of play, does not necessarily exclude the use of the 3-point shot. It does mean considerable planning must go into how players go about obtaining 3-point shots. Particular emphasis must be placed on teaching shot selection.

Number 60

Be True to What You Believe as a Coach

Every coach will have preconceived ideas of how the game should be played when starting a career in coaching. Over time those ideas may change or be reinforced due to experience. Regardless, coaches should never abandon a closely held principle or idea that is important to how the coach thinks the game should be played unless the coach either has good reason to do so or has made a reasoned decision to do so.

Coaches are all too often guilty of adopting the offense or defense of a team who made a deep run into the NCAA tournament without really learning the system of play, how to teach the system and if the coach has the personnel to play the system. Even worse, the coach may be adopting a system that violates how the coach thinks the game should be played.

If a coach believes deliberate offense and taking care of the ball each possession is a core offensive value, suddenly adopting a style of play that involves fast break offense and shooting a large number of 3-point shots is setting up the coach, program and players up for failure.

A change in style of play means adopting new strategy and tactics, developing a different understanding of how time and score applies. New tactics mean a new approach to teaching the game.

If you believe the 3-point shot should be used sparingly, then that is how you should coach. Any other approach would ultimately lead to disastrous results. Be true to what you believe as a coach.

12

General Tactics for Obtaining the 3-Point Shot

Number 61

The Concept of Offensive Building Blocks

Every offense is based around "offensive building blocks." Offenses are made of basic fundamentals such as passing, dribbling, cutting and screening. When combined in particular combinations, these become "building blocks." A down screen is one such example. Dribble penetration for the purpose of scoring a lay-up or drawing a defender, a penetrate and pitch, is another example of a building block. When these various building blocks are combined an offensive system is created. Some building blocks are general in nature and others are specific to attacking man-to-man or zone defense.

Number 62

Screen the Defense

Moving the ball and moving players are all forms of offensive movement and if done with proper spacing and timing, can be problematic for any defense. If these are the only offensive tactics, or building blocks, utilized, sound, well coached and hustling defenses can easily defend these tactics. Add screening to the mix and even the best defenses have to adjust and increase their level of intensity to defend the offense.

Number 63

Be a Second Cutter

Defenses work very hard to successfully defend the first cutter, the offensive player who uses the screen to get open. Where defenses are vulnerable is not in covering the initial screen but in defending the second cutter. The offensive player who set the screen is often more likely to be the player who will be able to get open for a shot.

To be an effective second cutter the screener must set a solid, legal screen forcing his/her defender to give help on the first cutter. The screener then executes a rear turn and shows his/her numbers to the ball. Sometimes this is enough to be open for a pass or a shot. In other instances the second cutter must cut in a direction opposite (**Diagram 63-A**) or at a 90-degree angle to the cut of the first cutter (**Diagram 63-B**).

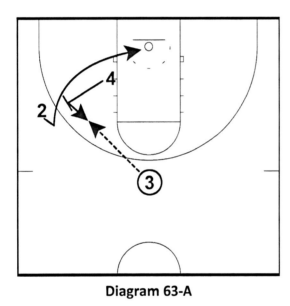
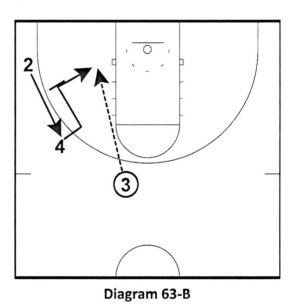

| Diagram 63-A | Diagram 63-B |

Number 64

Penetrate and Pitch

Dribble penetration is an outstanding offensive tactic in creating scoring opportunities. If the defense does not react to stop the dribble penetration the offensive player driving the lane will score a lay-up. The dribble penetration action forces the defense to rotate in order to prevent the easy lay-up, leaving another offensive player open for a shot opportunity. For the penetrate and pitch tactic to work effectively, the offensive players involved must recognize the dribble penetration and move to areas where a pass away from the defense can be made.

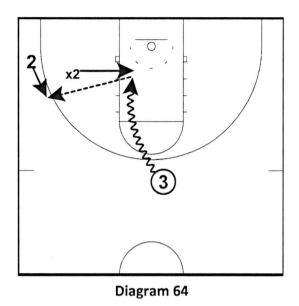

Diagram 64

Number 65

Penetrate and Skip

Penetrate and skip is a tactic similar to penetrate and pitch. Penetrate and pitch nearly always involves penetration down the middle to draw a defensive player. Penetrate and skip involves penetration from the wing to draw a help side defender from an offensive player on the opposite side of the court.

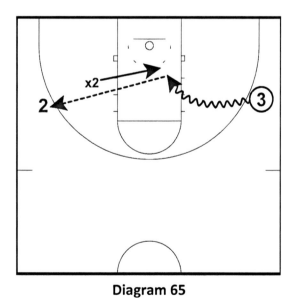

Diagram 65

Number 66

Baseline Drift

As a general rule, driving baseline is an offensive tactic that may force the defense to react, but it does so in an area where the defense is strong and designed to react in a way to create maximum defensive protection around the goal. The defense also has the added advantage of the baseline acting as an extra defender, limiting the area where the offense can operate. Middle penetration is more effective due to the stress it places on the defense's ability to rotate successfully and in a manner that allows the defense to recover effectively.

A baseline drift involves the help side offensive wing recognizing the fact the ball side wing is going to drive baseline. The help side wing "drifts" to the corner when the ball is driven baseline, creating a passing lane for the penetrating player. The offense must recognize any defender who could rotate into the passing lane as a part of normal defensive rotation. One tactic that will reduce turnovers is to pass the ball away from all defenders by passing the ball in the narrow lane behind the backboard but still inbounds. Defenders simply do not think to cover this area for possible passes, decreasing the chances for a turnover.

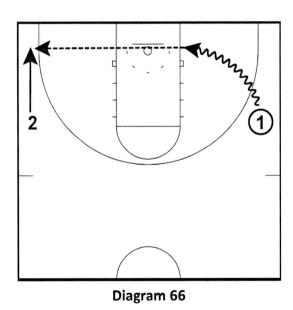

Diagram 66

Number 67

Euro

This tactic simple yet effective tactic was developed in Europe, hence the name "Euro" or "International." The ball handler penetrates the 3-point line, forcing the defense to either rotate to prevent the lay-up or stay home on the perimeter shooter to prevent giving up the 3-point shot. The perimeter player located in the direction the ball handler is driving must rotate to the area directly behind the penetrating ball handler. The ball handler executes a jump stop, rear turn or pivot, effectively sealing the defense and passes the ball back to the open 3-point shooter (**Diagram 67-A**).

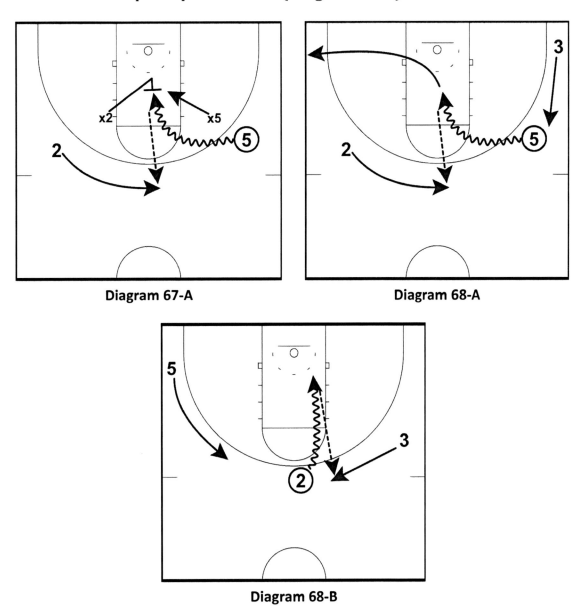

Diagram 67-A   **Diagram 68-A**

Diagram 68-B

Number 68

Double Euro

The "Double Euro" is the Euro tactic repeated twice in succession (**Diagram 68-A**). The Double Euro is difficult to defend as it requires the defense to successfully help and recover quickly twice in succession. The key to this tactic being successful is proper spacing, the ability of the perimeter players to penetrate, jump stop, rear turn (pivot), seal the defense and pass to the open player who must read the Euro opportunity and cut to the open area behind the penetrating ball handler. Once the ball handler has passed the ball handler must cut to the open area on the perimeter to create space and balance the offensive court (**Diagram 68-B**).

13

Tactics and Offensive Building Blocks for 3-Point Man-to-Man Offense

Number 69

Down Screen

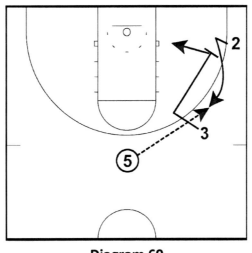

Diagram 69

Off all the basic offensive building blocks, the down screen is one of the most simple to implement. In **Diagram 69** #3 cuts to the line between the offensive player with the ball and the player to be screened for. #3 motions to #2 that he/she is going to screen for #2. #2 waits for the screen to be set. #3 sets a legal screen, making contact with the defender of #2, not the empty space, and remains stationary. #2 waits until the screen has been set, executes a v-cut to set the defender into the screen and rubs shoulders with the screener when coming off the screen. #2 must have hands up ready to receive the pass, face-up, look under the net and possibly shoot.

Number 70

Flare Screen

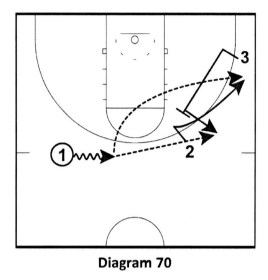

Diagram 70

The flare screen is utilized to get players open on the perimeter wings. The screener is positioned on the wing, below the intended cutter. #3 signals to #2 a flare screen will be set. #3 must leave one step between the defender and the screen so a foul will not be called. #3's back must be facing the corner to establish the correct angle for the screen. #2 must v-cut to set the screen, rub shoulders with the screener and face the basket with hands ready to catch and knees bent ready to shoot. (See **Diagram 70**)

Number 71

Pin Screen

Diagram 71

The pin screen is an effective tool to create a large amount space for the shooter. The pin screen is particularly effective against teams who play excellent help side defense, positioning help defenders guarding perimeter players two or more passes away from the ball in the lane area to congest the lane and help defend the offensive low post (**Diagram 71**). In the example shown #4 "pins" #3's defender, X3, into the lane, allowing a quick skip pass to #3 create an open 3-point shot. #4 can act as a second cutter by sealing X3 in the lane and posting up for a post entry pass from #3 if X4 closes-out to prevent the 3-point shot attempt.

Number 72

Re-Screen

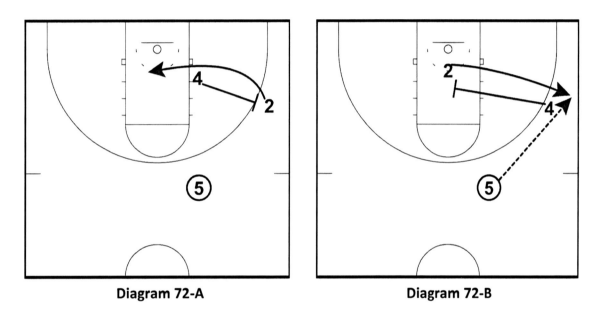

Diagram 72-A	Diagram 72-B

Rescreening is an excellent tactic to create shots. Multiple, successive screens is difficult to defend. There are multiple ways to rescreen a defender. In **Diagram 72-A** #4 sets a back screen for #2. After shaping up to be a second cutter, #4 sets a pin screen for #2 who did not receive a pass on the back door cut. After pin screening for #2, #4 should seal and post if #2 does not have a good 3-point shot opportunity (**Diagram 72-B**).

Common combinations for rescreen opportunities include down screen followed by a flare screen, flare screen followed by a down screen and a pin screen followed by a back screen.

Number 73

Drive Against the Grain

Driving against the grain is an outstanding one-on-one tactic. **Diagram 73-A** depicts the offensive player #3, making a long v-cut to get open. Note the distance the defender, X3, must cover.

Diagram 73-B depicts #3 "driving against the grain." This means the offensive player drives in the direction from which he/she initially cut. In this example, this means #3 drives back to the left hand low post block.

This tactic works because of the Law of Inertia. An object in motion tends to stay in motion and travel in a straight line (the direction the object was initially traveling in). Note X3's momentum carries him/her in the direction opposite of where #3 will drive.

To make this tactic most effective, #3 must attempt to catch facing the goal in triple threat ready to shoot a 3-point shot. A two-inch shot fake, combined with a crossover, make the initial attack almost impossible to defend, forcing the defense to rotate to help. This is an excellent attack for slower offensive players to initiate dribble penetration. For 3-point shooters who will be pressured on the perimeter, this is an essential skill to add to the arsenal.

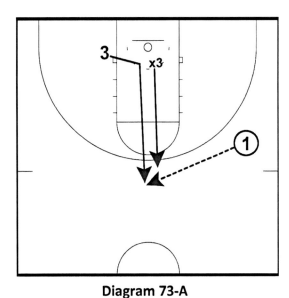

Diagram 73-A

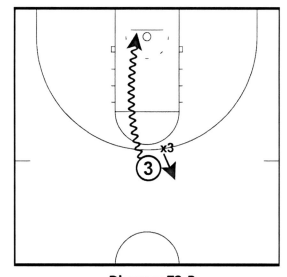

Diagram 73-B

The drive against the grain sequence: catching the pass, squaring up in triple threat, two-inch shot fake and then an attacking crossover step from the direction the cutter came from. Photographs by Maddy Copello

Receiving the Ball

Face-up

Two-inch Shot Fake

Crossover Step Against the Grain

14

General Tactics for Zone Attack Offense

Move the Ball and Move People

Number 74

Always Assertively Face-up and Look Under the Net

With the possible exception of a low post offensive player, every single time an offensive player receives the ball, the player must without fail face-up and look under the net. This habit allows the offensive player to see all four teammates as well as all five defensive players.

This habit allows the offensive player to take advantage of open teammates, potential defensive mistakes and scoring opportunities. Failure to assertively face-up allows the defense to pressure the ball into possible turnovers and the offensive player is not able to attack the defense by pass, drive or shot.

Number 75

All Zone Defenses Key Off the Ball

Man-to-man defense can be described as one defender guarding the ball and four defenders helping. Zone defense is five defenders guarding the ball and a specified area of the court. For a zone defense to be effective, it must work this way. In fact, this is a strength of zone defense.

Like most things though, a strength can also be a weakness. Because the zone keys on the ball, the offense can set up attacking tactics behind the zone or use fakes to freeze or shift the zone.

Number 76

Move the Ball With a Purpose

One of the worst habits players can develop on offense is to move the ball with no specific purpose in mind. This is particularly true in regard to the use of the dribble.

The ball should only be moved with a specific purpose in mind. The following are six acceptable reasons to move the ball in a zone offense by pass or dribble:

- To score.
- To improve passing angle.
- To feed the post.
- To distort the zone defense.
- To take advantage of a potential scoring opportunity two passes away.
- To escape trouble.

Number 77

Move the Ball to Distort the Zone

Regardless of the zone defense, all want to defend specific areas of the court and to do so in specific ways. Distorting the zone by moving defenders out of their assigned areas creates gaps and rotational problems for zones.

Dribbling the ball off the baseline when pressured by a backline defender of a 2-3 zone will create a gap on the baseline for a shooter to slip into. Passing the ball into the short post area will force the defense to change its zone slides to cover the ball.

Number 78

Move People to Distort the Zone

Just as moving the ball can cause a zone defense to distort, so can moving people. Initial alignments are one way to distort a zone. Lining up post players deep in the court near the offensive team's goal will force all zone defenses to either back up from the initial desired defensive areas or to spread the zone out vertically, creating larger than normal gaps in the zone defense.

Number 79

Move People Into the Gaps

All offensive systems want open players to receive the ball, either for open shots or the ability to face-up and pass the ball without defensive pressure on the ball. Placing players in gaps or moving players into gaps in zone defenses make this goal more easily achievable for zone offenses. It has the further benefit of possibly distorting the zone defense from its desired positions.

Number 80

Flash Cutters From Behind the Zone Into the Gaps

Take advantage of the zone defense's need to maintain constant visual contact with the ball and its location. Timed flash cuts into gaps from behind the line of vision of the zone defenders gives the offense the added advantage of the element of surprise.

This is one of the key reasons why all offensive players must assertively face-up and look under the net after receiving the ball. Failure to do so will rob the offense of the brief opportunity available to pass the ball to a cutter moving into a gap from behind the zone.

As the cutter moves into the open area of the zone defense, the cutter also moves into the visual line of sight of the defenders, allowing the defenders to adjust their position accordingly. The flash cutter will usually be open briefly, requiring a well-timed pass to the flash cutter.

Number 81

Use Shot Fakes to Freeze the Zone

One of the most effective weapons against any zone defense, and one of the least used, is the ball fake. A two-inch shot fake will momentarily freeze the zone defense due to the zone's fixation with the ball. This one second may be all that is required to give a cutter time to move into an open area, allow a screen to be set or for an offensive player to move into position to score.

Note, if the offensive player with the ball is not facing the basket, the shot fake will not be believable and will not achieve the desired effect of freezing the zone.

Number 82

Use Pass Fakes to Shift the Zone

Just as a shot fake will freeze a zone, an excellent pass fake that is believable capable of shifting all five zone defenders in the direction of the pass fake.

This can create openings in the zone, relieve pressure on the ball or force the defense into poor position to recover. For a pass fake to be believable there must be an offensive player in the general area of the pass fake.

Number 83

Change Direction

Combining a pass fake or shot fake with a change of direction of the movement of the ball can force the zone defense into poor position and create problems when the defense recovers. This is a particularly useful concept against zone defenses that are well coaches and aggressive in moving as a unit.

An example of effective use of this tactic would be for an excellent three-point shooter located on a wing to pass the ball to a teammate on the top of the key area. This teammate takes one hard dribble away from the three-point shooter towards the other wing, pass fakes to the wing and passes back to the three-point shooter.

While the ball was being dribbled off the top, the former ball side low post offensive player moved up the lane and set a flare screen on the back of the zone.

The extra few feet created by shifting the zone and the one or two seconds obtained by the pass fake and one dribble is often all that is needed to obtain an excellent shot for the three-point shooter (**Diagram 83**).

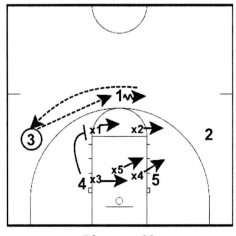

Diagram 83

Number 84

Use Skip Passes

Most well coached defenses are good at providing help. This is not where the defense is usually beaten by the offense, recovery from providing help is.

Skip passes are an excellent way to force the defense to cover long distances in recovery. Mistakes in closing out or positioning can be taken advantage of by forcing the defense to cover long distances. If the defense is forced to move twelve feet at maximum speed in recovery, the offense can use the defense's momentum against individual defenders This is done by driving in the direction opposite of where the defender came from, usually towards the goal.

Number 85

All Zones Become a 2-3 Zone

All zone defenses morph into some form of a 2-3 zone when the ball is moved to the corner, if the zone defense pressures the ball. This is worth being aware of for a variety of reasons. Care must be taken to teach players about the strengths and weaknesses of the 2-3 when the ball is in the corner, particularly odd front zones.

Odd front zones are vulnerable to the diagonal skip pass from the corner once in the 2-3 zone alignment. Even front zones are vulnerable to a skip pass on top followed by a direct dribble attack.

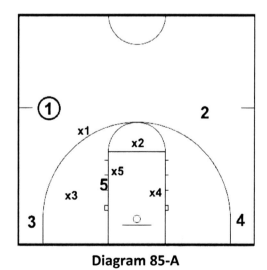

Diagram 85-A

Diagrams **85-A** and **85-B** depict the normal slides of an aggressive 2-3 zone defense that both pressures the ball and wants to eliminate ball reversal.

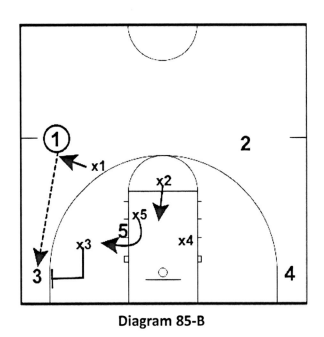

Diagram 85-B

Diagram 85-C depicts an aggressive 2-3 zone positioned to pressure the ball and eliminate ball reversal. X3 is applying pressure to the ball and X1 is denying the direct pass back to #1. This aggressive attitude and positioning creates pressure while disrupting easy movement of the ball on the perimeter.

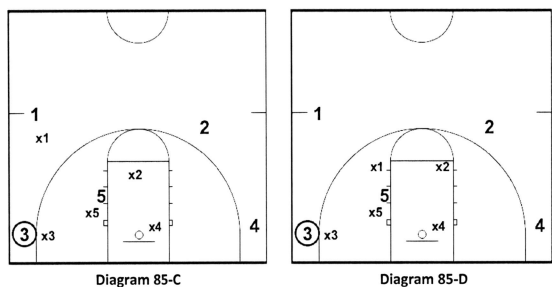

Diagram 85-C   Diagram 85-D

Diagram 85-D depicts a more passive 2-3 zone. The ball is being pressured but more emphasis is being placed on protecting the high post. The defense is willing to allow the offense to reverse the ball with a pass.

So what is the big deal? Why is this piece of information important? Forcing zones to alter their basic shifts and slides, making the defense do something it does not want to is a key principle in attacking any zone defense.

Assertive defenses do not want ball reversal and all defenses are vulnerable if the ball penetrates the defense, either by pass or dribble. Passive defenses protect the post and lane areas and are specifically designed to prevent penetration by pass or dribble.

Having the knowledge and ability to immediately hurt either of these types of defenses forces the opponent to be reactive from the start of the game, giving the offense a distinct advantage. The defense will have to reveal its adjustments to these tactics immediately and abandon its normal defensive style of play early in the game.

Diagram 85-E depicts the diagonal skip pass attack against an assertive 2-3 zone alignment. The attack should begin with a pass fake to #1 to freeze the defense momentarily. #2 adjusts to the open gap the defense presents with its positioning.

Upon catching the ball #2 may either shoot a three-point shot or shot fake the defender X2 and drive the lane line, forcing X4 to help, creating either a baseline jump shot or a three-point attempt for #4. #5 seals X5 out of the lane and is available for a pass as well from either #2 or #4 if X4 is able to react to the pass to #4 (**Diagrams 85-E** through **8-H**). Note in **Diagram 85-H** #1 and #3 are moving to floor balance.

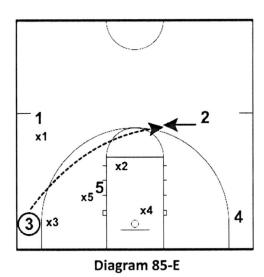
Diagram 85-E

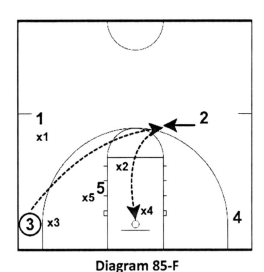
Diagram 85-F

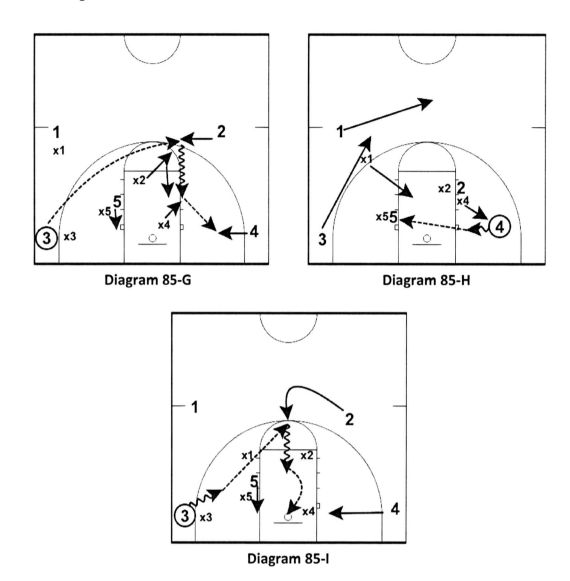

Diagram 85-G

Diagram 85-H

Diagram 85-I

Attacking a more passive zone defense is shown in **Diagram 85-I**. #2 has slipped right into the gap in the zone defense. #3 freezes the defense with a short dribble penetration and passes to #2.

#2 has the option of shooting the three-point shot, shot faking and driving for a score or a pass to either #4 or #5 (**Diagrams 85-I** through **85-L**). Note in **Diagram 85-L** #1 and #3 are moving to floor balance.

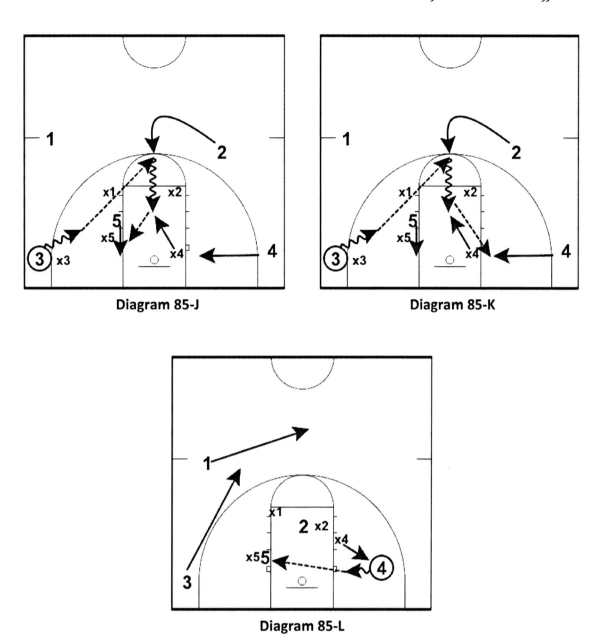

Diagram 85-J

Diagram 85-K

Diagram 85-L

Knowing all zone defenses morph into a 2-3 zone when the ball is moved to the corner allows a zone offense to be ready to attack and place the defense at a disadvantage the first offensive possession of the game the opponent deploys a zone defense, regardless of the type of zone defense.

How do the common zone defenses morph into a 2-3 zone? **Diagrams 85-M** through **85-T** depict the shifts and are labeled to identify the type of zone defense deployed as well.

67

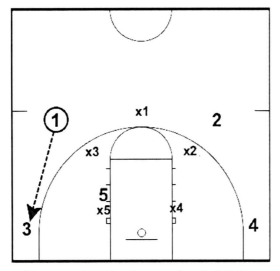

Diagram 85-M – Aggressive 1-2-2 Zone

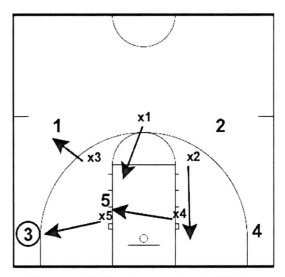

Diagram 85-N – Aggressive 1-2-2 Zone

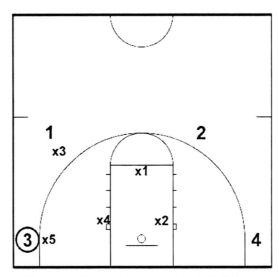

Diagram 85-O – Aggressive 1-2-2 Zone

Examine **Diagram 85-O** and **Diagram 85-C**. There is no difference in the areas being defended, only a difference in the players responsible to defend a specific area. The aggressive 1-2-2 zone morphed into a 2-3 when the ball was passed to the corner.

Examine **Diagram 85-Q** and **Diagram 85-D**. The passive 1-2-2 zone morphed into a passive 2-3 zone. Again, the same areas of the court are defended with only the players defending the area changing.

Diagram 85-R through **Diagram 85-T** depict a 1-3-1 zone. Compare **Diagram 85-S** and **Diagram 85-C**. The assertive nature of the 1-3-1 zone causes it to morph into a 2-3 when the ball is moved to the corner. The 3-2 zone and 1-1-3 are not depicted due to their similarity to the 1-2-2 and 2-3.

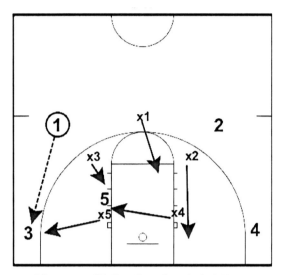

Diagram 85-P – Passive 1-2-2 Zone

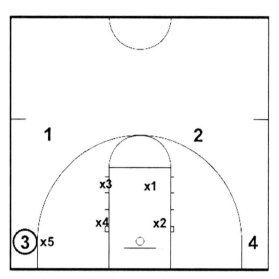

Diagram 85-Q – Passive 1-2-2 Zone

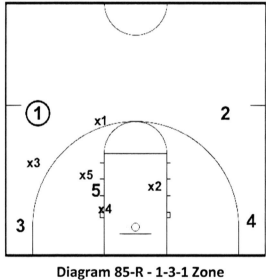

Diagram 85-R - 1-3-1 Zone

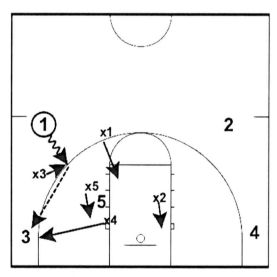

Diagram 85-S – 1-3-1 Zone

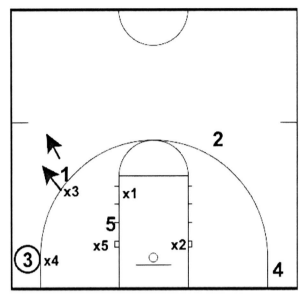

Diagram 85-T – 1-3-1 Zone

15

Offensive Building Blocks for 3-Point Zone Attack Offense

Number 86

Loop

The dribble loop can be used to create a variety of opening as well as to move the ball to the wing if the zone defense is making a point to wing pass difficult. **Diagram 86-A** depicts a dribble loop without any defenders for the purpose of clarity.

The ball handler dribbles directly at the player intended to make the loop cut. The cutter makes a curved cut underneath the ball handler being careful to create sufficient space as depicted and always facing the ball and maintaining eye contact with the ball handler. The ball handler, upon reaching the wing, faces-up and rips the ball across his or her chest and passes with the outside hand away from the defense to the loop cutter on top.

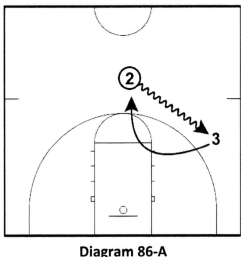

Diagram 86-A

Diagram 86-B shows the defensive action of a 2-3 zone against a loop cut. The backline defenders have been omitted for clarity. X2 maintains pressure on the ball as #s drives towards the wing initiating the dribble loop.

X1 shifts over to cover the ball side high post area while #3 loop cuts underneath the dribble and immediately faces-up upon arrival at the top of the three-point circle. The simple dribble loop alone may be enough to obtain a three-point shot. If a seam in the zone is available a high low ball side low post feed can be made as well.

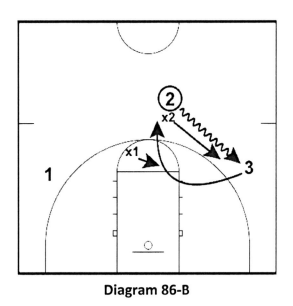
Diagram 86-B

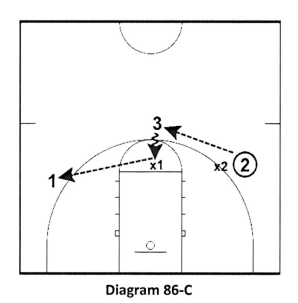
Diagram 86-C

A hard dribble at X1 will freeze the defender allowing a pass to the open shooter on the wing. Often this will result in an open three-point shot or as X1 sprints to close out an additional opportunity to penetrate the zone with a pass or dribble drive (**Diagram 86-C**).

Number 87

Loop and Screen-in

Zone defenses are based on two basic concepts. Every defender shifts based on the location of the ball and each defender is responsible for a specific area of the court to defend. The loop and screen-in tactic purposefully takes advantage of these to concepts.

The looping action focuses the defense's attention on the ball and shifts the zone away from the 3-point shooter, in this case #2, who slides behind the zone defense while #4 quietly sets a screen-in against the deepest zone defender. #3 creates space by looping to the top when #1 dribbles at #3, hence the name dribble loop. #1 skip passes to #2 for a 3-point shot (**Diagram 87-A**). If the defense hustles and successfully covers the 3-point shot this is also an excellent tactic to enter the ball into the high or low post. See **Diagram 87-B**.

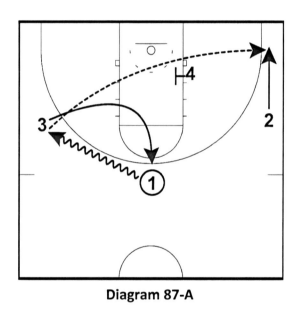

Diagram 87-A

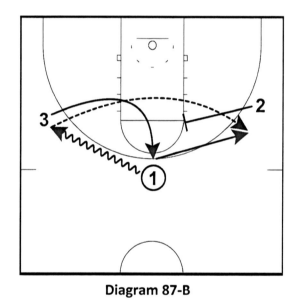

Diagram 87-B

Number 88

Loop Flare

The loop flare is similar to the loop and screen-in. The tactic is initiated with a dribble loop. Instead of a post player screening in, the help side perimeter player sets a flare screen for the looping perimeter player who has created space for the ball handler dribbling to the wing (**Diagram 88**).

Number 89

Skip Pass

The simple skip pass is often all that is needed to obtain a 3-point shot against a zone defense. A wise 3-point shooter knows when the ball is taken away from his/her side of the court, the defense may lose track of the shooter's location. Spotting up in a shooting stance ready to receive a pass speeds up a shot without rushing it. The attentive passer who sees the ready shooter in a seam of the zone on the opposite side of the court can make a crisp skip pass for the open 3-point attempt.

Number 90

Freeze and Slide

The first priority of all defensive systems is to stop the ball. Dribbling directly at a defender in a zone defense will force the defensive player to guard the ball in an effort to stop the ball from penetrating. The drive directly at the defensive player requires the defender to "freeze" in place in order to block the direct path of the attacking ball handler in the attempt of dribble penetrating directly to the goal.

Once the defensive player has been "frozen," the natural tendency of all defensive players is to now defend the ball so long as the ball handler continues to dribble the ball. This tendency should be taken advantage of by dribbling the zone defender away from his or her designated area of zone defense, either creating a gap, distorting the zone or forcing another defender to cover the newly opened gap in the zone, creating yet another distortion of the zone (**Diagram 90**). This concept is referred to as freeze and slide.

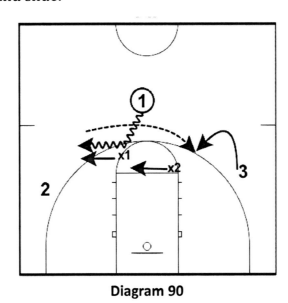

Diagram 90

Number 91

Dribble Off the Baseline

Baseline zone defenders are vulnerable to the dribble off tactic when the ball handler in possession of the ball is an excellent 3-point shooter. The nearest baseline defender must go out and pressure the ball or concede an easy 3-point attempt.

The shooter dribbles the ball assertively off the baseline using two dribbles, faces-up to the basket and pass fakes towards the next perimeter offensive player in the direction the ball handler
was dribbling or a teammate in the high post. This freezes the baseline defender for a second.

While the dribble off has been taking place a cutter from behind the zone has been moving towards the now unoccupied ball side corner (**Diagram 91-A**). The ball handler rips the ball across his or her chest and passes the ball away from the on ball defender to the cutter now occupying the corner (**Diagram 91-B**).

Often a single dribble off can create enough space and time for a good three-point shot. If X4 is a hard working defender X4 might be able to recover to the shooter who has just occupied the corner. If this is the case, immediately repeat the dribble off. Seldom is a defense able to defend this tactic twice in a row without making an adjustment to the basic zone defense's coverage.

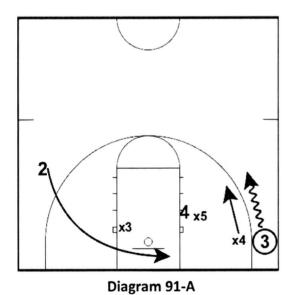

Diagram 91-A

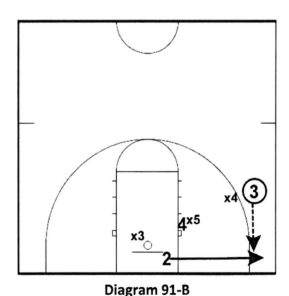

Diagram 91-B

Number 92

Dribble Off the Top

Dribbling the ball off the top of the three-point circle when combined with an effective pass fake can draw the top defenders of the zone in the direction the ball handler was dribbling. If the defense has shifted enough a three-point shot is possible. This tactic can also create gaps or seams for a pass from the perimeter player who received the initial pass to a flash cutter or post player (**Diagram 92**).

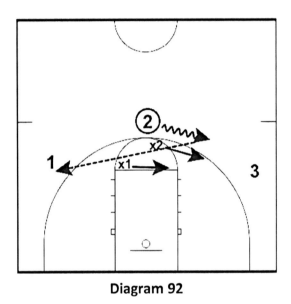

Diagram 92

Number 93

Penetrate and Skip

Penetrate and skip is a concept that combines penetration via the dribble with a skip pass. This combined tactic takes advantage of a gap in the zone and the fact a penetrating drive will draw or freeze zone defenders in place. The skip pass creates a long recovery situation for the zone and creates the possibility of a 3-point shot attempt, further penetration on the dribble or a pass in a gap created by the long recovery of the help side zone defenders (**Diagram 93**).

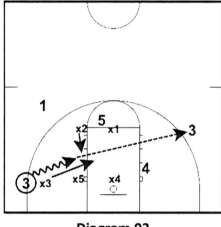

Diagram 93

Number 94

Dribble Follow

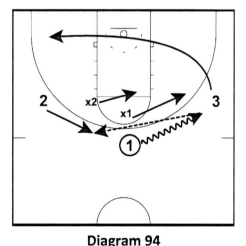

Diagram 94

The "Dribble Follow" is based on the premise of all five zone defenders defending an area and adjusting to the ball, a defensive tactic that requires all five defenders follow the movement of the ball. As depicted in **Diagram 94**, one player dribbles away and another follows into the open area created by moving the ball with the use of the dribble.

Number 95

Screen-in

Screening the zone is an effective yet seldom used tactic. The screen-in tactic is highly effective at setting up a three-point shot attempt and entering the ball into either the low post or high post. **Diagram 95-A** depicts the initial alignment against the backline of a 2-3 zone. For clarity the top two defenders have been omitted from the diagrams.

The wing opposite the ball, #2, slides down behind the low post opposite the ball. The ball is skip passed by #3 to #2 in the corner while #5 sets a legal back screen on the last defender of the zone defense (**Diagram 95-B**). If #2 has enough time, this will result in an excellent three-point shot opportunity.

When setting the back screen, not only does #5 have to give the defender being screened one step, the screen must be set at such an able the defender fights over the screen on the high side, or the side away from the baseline.

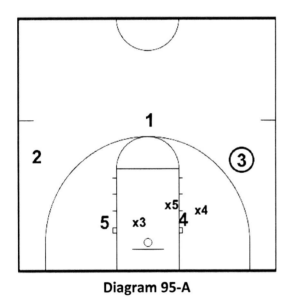
Diagram 95-A

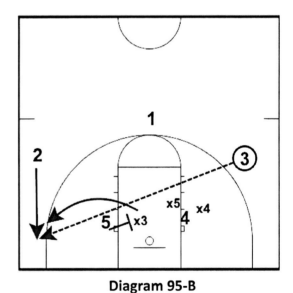
Diagram 95-B

The reason for setting the screen at this angle is to create plenty of space for a baseline bounce pass to enter the ball into the low post. After X3 fights over the screen from #5 and #5 goes to the next closest post defender and executes a rear turn (pivot) and seals the defender. The other offensive post player, #4, flashes into the ball side high post from behind the zone defense (**Diagram 95-C**). If #5 is open in the low post #2 makes the entry pass for a scoring opportunity.

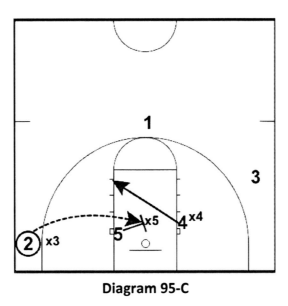

Diagram 95-C

If the ball is entered into the high post #5 changes the angle of the post seal to set up for a high low pass. The defender still must be pinned in the middle of the lane in order to create both a passing lane and a shot after catching the ball (**Diagram 95-D**).

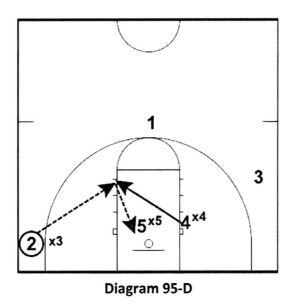

Diagram 95-D

Number 96

Flare Screen

Like the down screen, the flare screen is very similar as a flare screen set against man-to-man defense. Perimeter player #2 sets a flare screen on the last top zone defender X1. #1 makes a v-cut to utilize the flare screen, making certain his or her chest is facing the ball handler at all times.

   #3 drives the flare screen to freeze the defender being screened by taking one or two dribbles and then skip passing the ball to the cutter for a three-point shot attempt (**Diagram 96**).

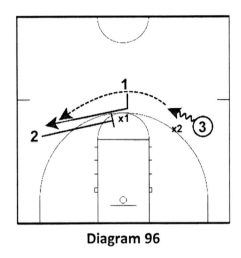

Diagram 96

Number 97

Screen Down

The screen down is very similar to setting a down screen against a man-to-man defense. The perimeter player at the top of the three-point line simply sets a down screen on the zone defender closest to the perimeter player opposite the ball. The perimeter player without the ball, #2, makes a v-cut to utilize the down and screen and receives the ball. The screener, #1, should balance the floor after setting the screen by filling what was #2's space on the court (**Diagram 97**).

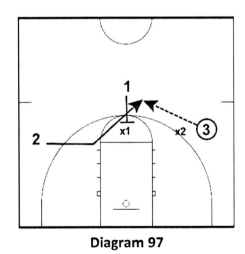

Diagram 97

16

Point Guard Play and the 3-Point Shot

Number 98

The Concept of Go To Move and Counter Move

While listed in the point guard section of this book, this principle applies to any position in the game of basketball and it applies to team strategy and tactics as well. Less is more!

Each player needs to develop a "go to" move and the appropriate counter move to compliment it. Lots of moves may look nice, but is this approach effective? Kareem Abdul Jabbar of the Milwaukee Bucks and Los Angeles Lakers signature move was the unstoppable skyhook. His counter move was to turn to the middle and shoot a short bank shot. The result, he retired as the all time leading scorer in the history of the game of basketball.

Great individual defensive players will attempt to force great 3-point shooters to put the ball on the floor as a primary defensive tactic. For 3-point shooters who have no counter move, this is a devastatingly effective defensive tactic!

What is the appropriate counter move for a 3-point shooter? The one dribble drive into the lane! The ability to use one dribble to drive the ball into the lane for a lay-up, a passing opportunity, pull-up mid-range jump shot or to execute a "Euro" creates so much havoc for the defense designed to force 3-point shooters to put the ball on the court the tactic will be either abandoned or rendered useless.

Number 99

Point Guards Create Opportunities for Their Teammates

Sadly, the pass first point guard is becoming a less common species in the game of basketball. Players seem to be enthralled with the idea of "getting theirs" and creating shots for themselves and not setting up their teammates. Post players are rendered helpless in this situation and great 3-point shooters are left with few scoring opportunities. Point guards are the coaches on the court. It is the point guard's job to create opportunities for teammates. Great point guards can control a game and never score a single point.

Number 100

The Counter Move for a Point Guard is the 3-Point Shot

Point guards should develop a 3-point shot as part of their individual arsenal. Just as the drive is the counter move for the great 3-point shooter, the 3-point shot is the counter move for the drive. Sound defensive teams facing a great penetrating point guard who cannot hit the 3-point shot will simply play off the point guard and "wall up" the lane, preventing penetration.

The 3-point shot as a counter move will force the defense to extend and pressure the point guard, once again creating opportunities for penetration to score and create scoring opportunities for teammates.

Number 101

Turn, Look, Decide and Go

Turnovers and missed opportunities by point guards are often the result of the point guard simply not "looking." These turnovers and missed opportunities can be eliminated by the point guard developing one simple habit.

Upon receiving the ball, the point guard must turn, look up the court under the net, observe both teammates and defenders, decide what to do and then go or act.

Number 102

Turn to the Middle

Upon receiving the outlet pass, the point guard must develop the habit of turning, looking, deciding and then going.

When turning, the point guard must always turn towards the middle of the court. This allows the point guard to see the maximum area of the court and see both the defenders and teammates.

Number 103

Dribble as Little as Possible

Good playmakers do not need to dribble a lot to be effective. In fact, the fewer dribbles taken, the less opportunity there is for a turnover and the sooner the ball will be in the hands of the of the open shooters!

Number 104

Practice Full Court Lay-ups at Game Speed!

Point guards, more than any other player, usually shoot lay-ups after driving full court and attacking the rim at maximum speed. Attackers will often shoot lay-ups at similar speeds. Often these lay-up attempts are missed, losing valuable points for the fast breaking team.

In order to develop the ability to make lay-ups at maximum speed, it is necessary to practice lay-ups at this speed. It is also necessary to replicate the distance covered at these speeds and develop the habit of taking the proper approach angle to the rim in order to obtain the highest possible field goal percentage.

This skill is an invaluable weapon in creating good 3-point shooting opportunities off the fast break. Even well organized defensive teams who demonstrate excellent defensive transition will collapse, leaving open 3-point shooters when faced with an attacking point guard capable of driving the length of the court and scoring.

Number 105

Limit of One Dribble from the 3-point Line to the Rim

Great penetrating attackers only need one dribble to make it from the 3-point line to the rim to shoot a lay-up. This offensive skill greatly enhances the ability of an offensive attacker to score, create opportunities for teammates, draw fouls and in general create problems for the defense. It will also cause many defensive players to give the offensive player considerable space to eliminate the attacking drive, creating opportunities for 3-point shots.

Number 106

Four Dribbles

Ball handlers should always be as efficient as possible with the use of the dribble. Just as the ball handler should drive from the 3-point line to the rim in one dribble, the ball handler should advance the ball up the court with the fewest number of dribbles possible.

An aggressive ball handler running at maximum speed can advance the ball up the court in four dribbles. Players who are not able to do this should work to develop this skill. Ball handlers who can advance the ball with just four dribbles are extremely difficult for the defense to stop in the open floor. This minimalist approach to advancing the ball with the dribble is not only difficult to defend, it creates numerous scoring and passing opportunities.

Weaker ball handlers, high school girls and middle school players should set an initial goal of five dribbles.

Number 107

Drive the Ball Into the Paint

All defensive systems are designed to protect the rim, the lane and then the 3-point line. Defenses are designed with help and recover concepts to prevent the ball from entering the low post or the lane.

With this in mind, the offense should always attack the very area the defense wants to protect the most. Point guards can create maximum opportunities for their team by driving the ball into the paint area and forcing the defense to collapse and then recover.

Number 108

Value the Assist!

More than anything else, a point guard should value the assist. This concept emphasizes the need to protect the ball and value possession of the ball. It also teaches the point guard to think with a servant's heart. This concept needs to be emphasized and reinforced by rewarding the point guard for assists by the coaching staff.

One of the best ways to reward assists is to emphasize the value of assists not just to the point guards on the team, but to every player in the program, generating the idea of assists as a high value statistic, as valuable as scoring points. This approach generates status among peers for high assist totals and removes some of the temptation to shoot instead of creating scoring opportunities for the team.

17

Perimeter Play and the 3-Point Shot

Number 109

The Majority of 3-Point Offensive Building Blocks Are Perimeter Based

While post players can shoot 3-pointers, and there are some very valid tactical and strategic reasons why post players should be trained to do so, the majority of offensive building blocks designed to obtain 3-point shots are perimeter based.

Number 110

Perimeter Offensive Building Blocks Are Skill Based

Regardless of the offense used, perimeter offensive building blocks are how most perimeter 3-point shots are generated. Since this is the case, perimeter players must master the basics of recognizing and utilizing these tactics. In addition, the fundamental skills of executing the cutting, screening, using screens, passing and catching is essential.

Number 111

Look for Seams

Defenses, particularly zone defenses, will have seams, or gaps in the defense. This is particularly true for offensive players on the help side of the court as the seams are formed in the help side defense. Perimeter players who are 3-point shooters must constantly be searching for seams to slip into. These seams can appear quickly and as the result of a tactics/building block like a penetrate and pitch, fanning the ball or a simple skip pass, requiring the 3-point shooter recognize the appearance of the seam and the tactic being used to take advantage of it.

Number 112

Look for Screeners and Shot Opportunities Combined

Moving the ball and moving players is hard enough for defenses to effectively cover. Adding screens to the equation is the most difficult offensive tactic for defenses to handle effectively on a consistent basis. The issue with screens and generating 3-point shots lies in the lack of recognition on the part of 3-point shooters and the offensive player in possession of the ball.

Shooters must be constantly looking for opportunities to get open. This means looking for teammates who are in position to set a screen, knowing where the ball is and who is in possession of the ball and knowing where and how the defense is defending. Knowing which teammate is likely to set a screen and where the screen will be set allows shooters to anticipate when, where and how to get open for a good shot. The essential key in all of this is recognition of the screening opportunity.

Number 113

Watch for Penetration

Just as 3-point shooters must look for screeners, shooters must look for penetration opportunities when not in possession of the ball. So many offensive building blocks are built around collapsing the defense with dribble penetration it is essential for shooters to maintain a constant awareness of any opportunities for penetration regardless of where the ball is located.

Penetration can occur from the middle (sets up Euros, Double Euros, penetrate and pitch) or the wing opposite the shooter (sets up penetrate and skip, baseline drift as well as some Euro opportunities. Penetration can take place in ways other than by dribbling. Passing the ball into the low post is a form of penetrating the defense and leads to opportunities to fan the ball for a 3-point shot.

Number 114

Have Your Hands Ready and Knees Bent

Shooters must be quick but not in a hurry. One of the best ways to shoot quickly without hurrying the shot is for the shooter to be squared up with knees bent and hands set in a correctly formed shooting pocket before the ball arrives. If the pass is pinpoint into the shooting pocket, half of the shooting motion is eliminated from the shot, allowing for a "quicker" shot without requiring the shooter to rush.

Number 115

The Two Inch Shot Fake is the Perimeter Player's Best Friend!

Of all the fundamental skills a shooter should have in his/her offensive arsenal, one of the least taught and used skills is the shot fake. The shot fake can freeze a defensive player, allowing the shooter to take a shot. The shot fake can fool a defensive player into making a critical mistake like leaving the court, allowing the offensive player to drive into the middle of the defense.

For shot fakes to be truly effective, two things must be executed correctly. First, the shooter must not allow the bend in the knees to be removed by standing up when shot faking. The most common cause of taking the bend out of the knees is a shot fake that is "too" long.

The correct length for a shot fake is a mere two inches. This is quick, sells the idea of a shot and does not risk removing the bend from the knees. If one shot fake does not work, the shooter should not despair, but instead, use another two inch shot fake.

18

Post Play and the 3-Point Shot

Number 116

Must Be Good Enough to Draw Two Defenders

One of the best measuring sticks to evaluate how effective a post player is on offense is the number of defenders required to prevent the post from scoring. If the post player can be defended with a single defender, the post can be considered as not very effective on offense. A post player is defended by two or more defenders is an effective offensive threat.

Post players who draw two defenders force the defense to leave on offensive player unguarded. Often the player used to "double" or "play behind" the post player is a perimeter defender who is playing help side defense. This often means a 3-point shooter is left unguarded on the opposite side of the court, open for a skip pass, a diagonal fan pass or a penetrate and skip.

Number 117

Teams Do Not Have to Have Post Players to Post Up

It is nice to have traditional back to the basket post players who are all tall, physical and possess excellent post skills. Not every team is so fortunate. This does not mean a team has to do without post play. Many small players, guards in fact, like to play in the post and can be quite effective. Consider cutting or flashing perimeter players into the post.

Bigger post defenders often cannot defend, smaller, quicker players. While not able to overwhelm a larger post defender with size and strength, perimeter players can use quickness to get around them and their passing skills will be of tremendous value in fanning the ball out to 3-point shooters on the perimeter.

Number 118

Fan the Ball

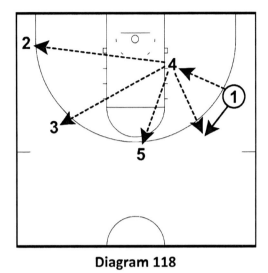

Diagram 118

The offensive low post is one of the best places on the court to pass the ball from. The proximity of the low post to the goal forces the defense to respect the location of the ball. An effective offensive low post player will force the opponent to use two or more defenders to cover the low post player when is possession of the ball.

Post players take time to develop effective offensive post moves. In addition to developing the ability to score in the low post, post players must be taught how to pass effectively from the low post.

Upon receiving the ball, the post player must chin the ball and check over the high shoulder (**Photograph 118-A**) before executing an offensive post move, unless the passer has "keyed" an open shot with the pass (for example, a bounce pass on the baseline side tells the post player a drop step is wide open). By checking over the high shoulder, the post player can see the majority of the court, locate the defenders and see open teammates.

The diagonal skip pass is the weapon of choice in this situation. The post player must square his/her shoulders to the shooter and step with the high side foot towards the target, if this foot has not been established as a pivot foot (**Photograph 118-B).** The post must use a two-hand overhead pass and pass away from the defense but directly to the shooting pocket of the shooter.

The shooter is the second half of this tactic and must move to create a clear passing lane for the post player, be ready squared up and ready to shoot with the knees bent and hands providing a shooting pocket as a target for the post player to pass to. The post player can also fan the ball back to the ball side perimeter who fed the post and then relocated to create an open passing lane.

Photograph 118-A
Photograph by Maddy Copello

Photograph 118-B
Photograph by Maddy Copello

Number 119

Feed the Post and Move

Teams will defend the offensive low post in a variety of ways. Some will double team from behind or on top. Others will play behind and collapse the ball side perimeter defenders on to the post player. If the post player is not particularly effective in scoring from the low post, many teams will use a single defender. All of these defensive tactics are vulnerable to "feed the post and move."

Diagram 119 demonstrates just how simple this tactic is. The perimeter player who feeds the post moves a minimum of 15 feet after passing the ball and prepares to shoot the 3-point shot upon catching a return pass. The post player chins the ball after receiving it, checks over the high side shoulder, reads the defense and passes the ball back to the perimeter player.

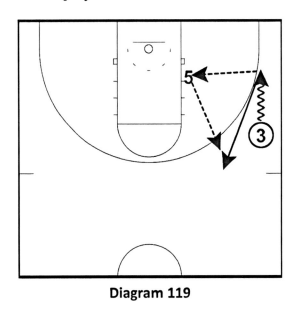

Diagram 119

Number 120

The "33" Cut

The "33" cut is a post player's dream. For the quick mobile post player who possesses good footwork, this tactic is an effective method to obtain good 3-point shots. The primary advantage of this tactic is the fact most post defenders are not particularly good perimeter defensive players.

The 33 cut is essentially a Euro. The perimeter player drives directly at the low post offensive player who loops around the driving perimeter player. The post player's defender must either stay home, respect the drive and give help or chase the offensive post player out to the perimeter, creating a lane for the driving perimeter player. If the driving perimeter player successfully draws the help of the post defender, the perimeter player jump stops, rear turns (pivots), chins the ball and passes out to the cutting post player for the 3-point shot (**Diagram 120**).

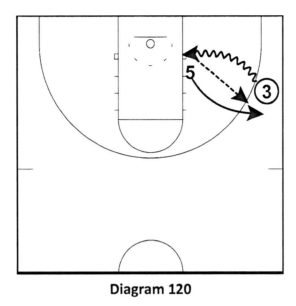

Diagram 120

Number 121

The "Long I-Cut"

Diagram 121-A shows an offensive post move utilizing a baseline drive by a perimeter player. The post player rear turns, steps to the front of the rim and the perimeter player makes a hook pass over the defense.

The Long I-Cut is a modification of this tactic. The post player sprints up the lane line and spots up for the 3-point shot. This tactic is only practical for quick and mobile post players (**Diagram 121-B**).

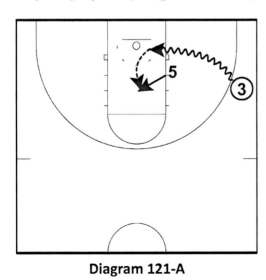

Diagram 121-A

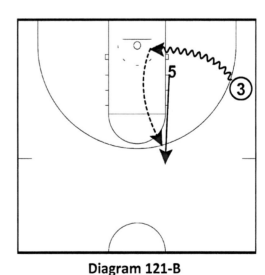

Diagram 121-B

19

The Fast Break and the 3-Point Shot

Number 122

Why Wait?

In times past I coached a very deliberate style of play. The goal was to play 24 minutes of motion offense and 8 minutes of ferocious man-to-man defense. We passed up good shots to get better shots and my teams were very good at this style of play. Coach Dick Bennett would have been proud. I then went to the other extreme, playing a Loyola Marymount style of play, adopting the "guru of go's" philosophy of "if you get a good shot in 5 or 6 seconds why wait?" This approach is not for the faint of heart but I have never looked back and for me, it was the right choice.

Unless time and score dictate a 3-point shot is the only acceptable shot, I still believe attacking the basket for a lay-up is how you win games. If there are no defenders or only one defender back, attack and score the lay-up. But if there are two defensive players back, the odds for obtaining a lay-up are dramatically reduced to the point where the wise choice is to run some offense.

Since most teams focus their defensive efforts against the fast break in stopping the ball and defending the rim, there will be countless good 3-point shot opportunities for the team who is organized and looking for a 3-point shot when there are two or more defensive players back.

Most teams will pull back their offensive attack and transition into half court offense. My question is why wait? If your style of play is a constant fast paced attack, why make five or six passes to obtain an open 3-point shot when the same shot is available after one or two passes?

Psychologically, it can be devastating for the opponent to sprint back to play defense and to be scored upon with in seconds. It is even worse when the field goal made is a 3-point goal followed up by an intense full court, pressing defense. The nature of the 3-point shot once shooters start hitting is a snowball effect can be created, especially when combined with pressing defense and a fast break attack.

Number 123

Consider a Numbered Break

Many coaches think an all out fast break attack is undisciplined. It can be. To be truly consistent and effective a fast break attack actually needs to be more disciplined than a deliberate, slow paced half court attack.

It is possible to run a rule based fast break similar to a motion offense. It is much easier to obtain the discipline required and provide excellent structure for shooters and penetrators to operate from by using a numbered fast break.

Essentially this approach involves assigning players specific fast break lanes to run and duties to perform. It also ensures the players will arrive at assigned spots on the court, guaranteeing proper spacing and the right player in the right position on the court.

Any coach interested in this approach should consider the breaks used by Paul Westhead of Loyola Marymount/LA Lakers NBA Champions fame, David Arsenault of Grinnell College and Doug Porter, coach of the Lady Tigers of Olivet Nazarene University.

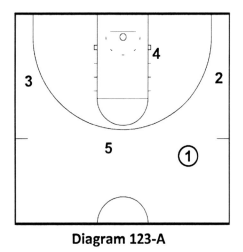

Diagram 123-A

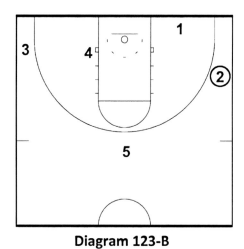

Diagram 123-B

The two diagrams above depict two different sets of "spots" a numbered fast break can finish with. **Diagram 123-A** depicts the common Loyola Marymount finish to the break and **Diagram 123-B** depicts the finish to the Olivet Nazarene break. Both have finishes have their advantages and disadvantages. The Loyola finish provides a ball side low post and excellent spacing but limits the penetration opportunities due to the location of the post player. The Olivet finish offers good offensive rebounding position and excellent penetration opportunities but has no immediate ball side low post to attack. **Diagram 123-C** depicts a numbered break run off a made basket from a 2-3 zone using the Olivet lanes.

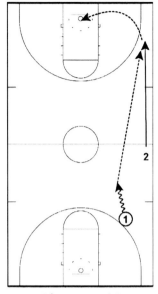

| Diagram 123-C | Diagram 124 |

Number 124

Pitch-a-Head

The fastest way to advance the ball up the floor for a good shot and to catch the opponent in poor defensive position is to "pitch-a-head." The quicker the pass across half court is made, the greater the advantage the offense will have. One of the best opportunities for a quick 3-point shot is a pitch-ahead to one of the attacking wings on the fast break (**Diagram 124**).

Number 125

Pull Up

The fastest way to start the fast break is for the point guard to obtain the defensive rebound or turnover and immediately fill the point guard lane. The fastest way to obtain a 3-point shot is to pitch-a-head to the 2 or 3 filling their lanes. The next fastest way, and the one way to make sure there is no turnover due to a bad pass is for the point guard to simply pull up for a 3-point shot.

When time and score is critical, simply having the point guard pull up for a 3-point attempt is a quick way and effective tactic if the point guard is capable of the shot.

Number 126

Use the Trailer

The trailer, usually post player and the designated inbounder in a numbered fast break, is almost always open. If this player can shoot the 3-point shot this is a particularly effective tactic (**Diagram 126-A**). It will force the defense to extend, opening up the high low pass to the low post (**Diagram 126-B**) and creating penetration opportunities for the trailer.

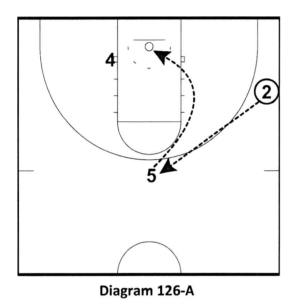 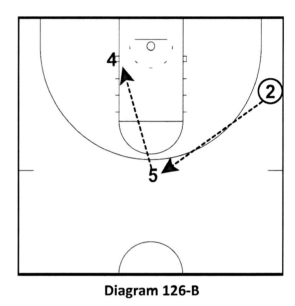

| Diagram 126-A | Diagram 126-B |

Number 127

Fan the Ball

Giving 3-point shooters a chance to lineup square to the goal before shooting increases their field goal percentage. One of the best ways to do this is to pass the ball from the inside out, or fanning the ball from the low post. Because defenses are trained to defend from the rim out, if the ball can be entered into the low quickly the defenders will be collapsed into the lane. When the ball is fanned out in this situation, the 3-point shooters will be provided with an extra second, allowing an unrushed shot to be taken.

Number 128

Use Offensive Building Blocks

My preferred system of attacking is to provide a basic structure for players to work from. The numbered break provides a starting point as the players advance up the court quickly and in a disciplined and organized manner, finishing in well established spots on the court. From these points on the court players can read the defense and make use of offensive building blocks they have mastered to attack and obtain good 3-point shot opportunities as well as opportunities to drive for lay-ups or to post up. Offensive building blocks that work well with the fast break include:

- skip pass
- penetrate and skip
- penetrate and pitch
- baseline drift
- Euro
- fan the ball
- dribble follow
- dribble off
- screen-in

Number 129

Better Offensive Rebounding Opportunities?!

Shooting quickly in the fast break attack can lead to better offensive rebound opportunities. The defense is often clogged under the rim in the lane or at times disorganized due to the quick rush up the court. The longer rebounds of missed 3-point shots combined with the poor positioning of the defense leads to increased opportunities for alert, hustling offensive teams.

Number 130

Secondary Breaks

Teams requiring more structure in their offensive attack at the end of the fast break should make use of set plays popularly known as secondary breaks. These plays make use of predetermined spots on court and are designed to attack either zone or man-to-man defenses. For more information on secondary breaks see Chapter 21.

20

Concepts and Drills for Practicing the 3-Point Shot

Number 131

Develop an Integrated System of Teaching of Skills, Concepts and Tactics

Like pieces of a puzzle, when each piece is in its place, the picture is complete. The same can be said of teaching the game of basketball. It does not matter what you the coach know, it matters what your players know and have mastered, the good basketball habits your players have established as a result of good teaching, hard work and repetition.

The best programs in any sport have an integrated system. Every concept taught to players fit both the overriding purpose of the program and the offensive and defensive systems. The terminology used fits like a glove and each drill teaches only concepts, skills and tactics that fit the overall grand scheme of the program. There is no wasted time in practice as a result and the very nature of the carefully crafted puzzle fitting together eliminates any possible doubt or indecision from creeping into the minds of the players during a game.

If the skill, concept, drill or tactic does not serve a clear purpose in the overall system, eliminate it. Less is more. Refine each item in the integrated system, insuring clarity and purpose.

Number 132

Select Drills Carefully and With Purpose

Many coaches have beloved drills that are a part of the daily practice regimen that should not be utilized. It could be a drill used by the coach's high school coach, college coach or a well-known coach.

Only utilize drills specifically designed to teach the fundamentals and concepts essential to the offensive system being utilized. Practice time used for drills that do not teach and reinforce fundamentals, concepts and habits essential to the system utilized is practice time that is wasted and lost forever.

Every coach is guilty of this from time to time and care must be taken to avoid making this mistake. Practice time must be treated as a valuable commodity.

Number 133

Execution of Fundamentals At Game Speed Is Essential

Fundamentals are key for any phase of the game for a player, and a team, to be successful. This is especially true for the offensive phase of the game. Well executed offense will yield open shots, clear driving lanes to the goal and the ability to score large amounts of points in a short period of time, so does the opportunity to make bad passes, travel or mishandle a ball. Players, and coaches, must understand this aspect of offensive basketball. The key to maximizing the positive aspects while negating or reducing the negative aspects is to mast the fundamentals at "game speed."

Number 134

Practice Against the Clock

The ability to play with a sense of urgency for the duration of the game is essential. One of the best ways to build this habit so this becomes the norm and not a source of stress for players during a game is to practice against the clock.

Every possible drill that can be run for time and in some way made competitive should be modified to include the time element. Creating a game-like atmosphere in practice allows players to adjust to the pressure of always pushing the break and playing with a sense of urgency.

Number 135

Fundamental Lines

Fundamental lines is a series of drills designed to practice essential fundamentals, provide a high number of repetitions in a short period of time, build intensity and force players to concentrate on execution. The drills shown in this section can be run from the baseline, the ideal location, or the sideline if space and numbers dictate. Players ideally are in groups of three with a ball but groups of four or five are acceptable.

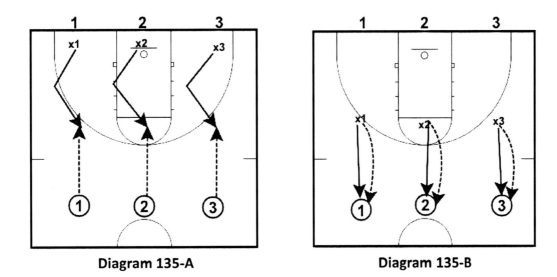

Diagram 135-A   Diagram 135-B

Diagrams 135-A and 135-B depict the drill sequence known as "easy running." This is drill is not meant to be performed at a high rate of speed and is a good warm-up for the more intense drills in this sequence. The first half of the sequence is shown in **Diagram 135-A** as the players on the baseline execute v-cuts. The passers are located near half court and pass to the cutter using their weak hand. Upon catching the pass, the cutter lands in triple threat and executes a weak hand pass back to the passer.

The cutter follows the pass to the passer and executes a jump stop into triple threat and takes an exchange from the passer, who is in triple threat with the ball, by pulling the ball from the grasp of the passer and then executing a rear turn. The passer moves out of bounds and hustles to the end of the cutter line on the baseline (**Diagram 135-B**).

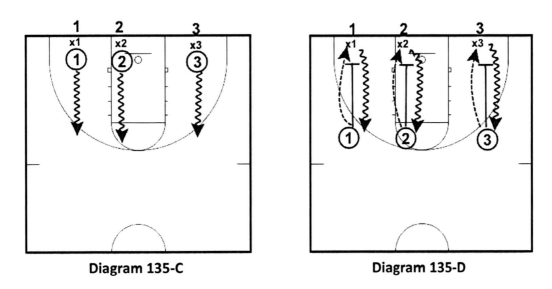

Diagram 135-C   Diagram 135-D

The next sequence in fundamental lines is "live ball." Transition to this second sequence by verbally calling "live ball." The player with the ball in each group, at that time, passes the ball to the first player in line, follows the pass and closes-out on the ball.

Diagrams 135-C and 135-D depict how the live ball series works. The first player in line executes a two-inch up fake or pass fake and then executes a long, low, straight start step, either a direct drive or a crossover. The player is to travel as far as possible with two dribbles, jump stop and execute a rear turn (pivot) in triple threat position. The player then passes the ball to the next player in line using a weak hand pass.

The player receiving the pass steps to the pass to shorten the pass. A good measure for a player or coach to determine if this happens is for the receiving player to be out of bounds when the pass is made and to catch the ball inbounds. The receiver catches the ball in triple threat position with a low, wide, base of balance and support.

The passer follows the pass and executes a defensive closeout. The receiver then executes a live ball move and takes two dribbles, executes a rear turn and makes a weak hand pass back to the next player. The sequence continues until the players are told to progress to the next series.

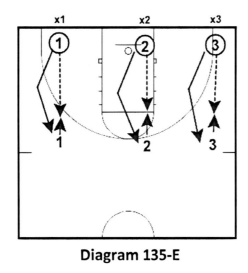

Diagram 135-E

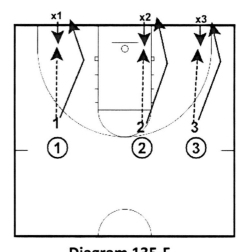

Diagram 135-F

Diagram 135-E depicts the start of the third, and most mentally challenging, phase of the fundamental lines series known as flick passing. Players transition from the live ball series by having a player execute the live ball move followed by two dribbles and pass the ball back to the first player on the baseline. This sequence must always start with the ball in the group of players with at least two players. The player who just executed the live ball move remains 15 to 18 feet away and awaits a return pass to start the sequence.

Following the transition from one drill to the next, the drill starts with the player with the ball on the baseline passing to the single player opposite. In the examples shown in **Diagrams 135-E and 135-F** the players are using a right hand pass to pass away from the defense.

All groups must start with the same pass. The passer follows the pass with a v-cut and a jump stop and rear turn behind the player who just received the ball. By starting the drill with all players using the same hand to pass with, collisions and injuries will be avoided.

The receiver must take a step to meet, or shorten, the pass. The receiver then repeats the procedure of the passer who initiated the drill. The drill continues until the coach gives the order to change hands being passed with. The drill continues without stopping, players simply change passing hands and the side to which players execute their v-cut. The key rule for players to remember for purposes of safety is to cut to the side of the hand the player passed with.

Number 136

Partner Lay-ups

Diagram 136-A depicts the basic pattern of Partner Lay-ups. The shooter, #1, drives for a lay-up. #2 rebounds the lay-up while #1 cuts hard to the other side of the court. #1 receives the pass by meeting the pass and assuming the triple threat position behind the three-point line. #1 then drives the basket again, repeating the process as depicted in **Diagram 136-B**. **Diagram 136-C** depicts how the shooter must vary the attack approach on each lay-up.

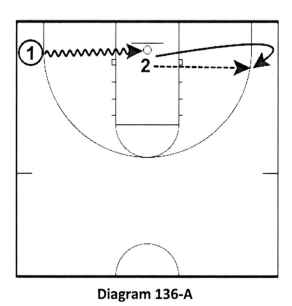

Diagram 136-A

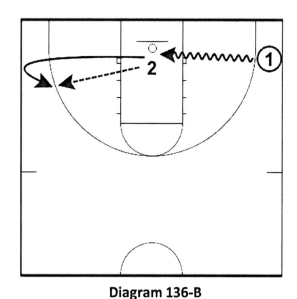

Diagram 136-B

Key coaching points include the following: the shooter tries to execute the drive with traveling with only one dribble, the ball must be shot high soft off the glass and the drive must be initiated from the triple threat position with a long, low start step.

The players work against the clock, starting with one minute and working up to 1.5 minutes. The rebounder keeps track of the number of made lay-ups and missed lay-ups. A target number of lay-ups for the players to make should be set prior to the start of the drill.

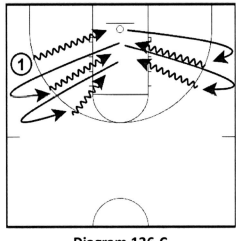

Diagram 136-C

Number 137

Basic Planning for 3-Point Shooting Drills

Diagram 137-A depicts the five primary shooting spots perimeter 3-point shooters should practice from. The spots can vary based on the needs of the offense being used. **Diagram 137-B** shows the area and spots post players who serve as trailers on the fast break must practice from to develop 3-point shooting ability.

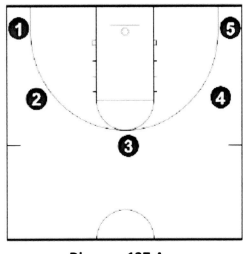

Diagram 137-A

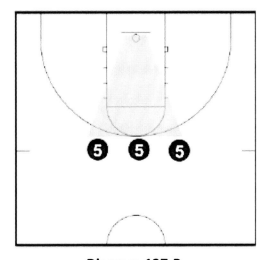

Diagram 137-B

Number 138

3-Point Shoot-out

This drill is designed to generate a high volume of 3-point shots in a short period of time. One to five shooters can work at a single time with five players rebounding, one designated rebounder for each shooter. Players shoot only from the five three-point shooting spots as indicated in **Diagram 138**. The drill should last for five minutes. Players are allotted one minute per spot after which the shooter rotates to the next spot. The rebounder keeps track of the number of shots made. At the end of the session the number of shots made should be recorded.

Diagram 138

Number 139

Partner Threes

Partner Threes is a simple concept for a drill. 3-point shooters are paired together for the duration of the drill and the sequences involved. One player executes the tactic being practiced and passes to the other player who has executed necessary moves to be open and ready to shoot upon catching the pass. The passer rebounds the shot and passes to the shooter. The two players then switch roles and repeat the process.

Players may shoot a preset number before moving on to the next series in the sequence or await the command of the coach. In **Diagram 139-A** the players are executing a penetrate and pitch. #1 drives the gap to draw #2's defender. #2 moves up from the baseline to create space and receive the pass from #1. #2 should have feet set, be squared-up, hands ready and prepared to shoot upon catching the pass.

The following diagrams demonstrate the various ways two players can create an open three-point shot attempt. The same drill procedure is used for the entire sequence. Please note an important component of the drill is not just the physical repetition of the skills involved and the tactic being practiced but also the ability to recognize the potential to create such a 3-point shot in a game by using one of the tactics being practiced.

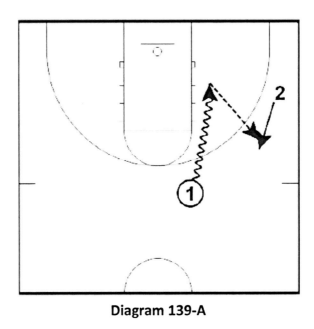

Diagram 139-A

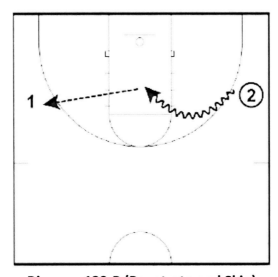

Diagram 139-B (Penetrate and Skip)

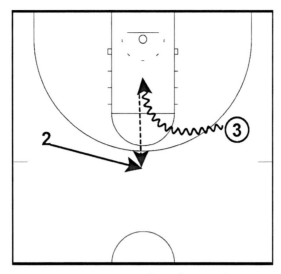

Diagram 139-C (Single Euro)

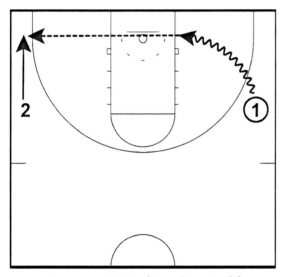

Diagram 139-D (Baseline Drift)

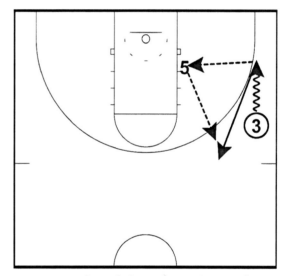

139-E (Feed the Post and Move)

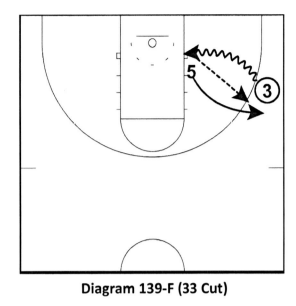

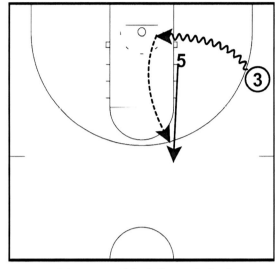

Diagram 139-F (33 Cut)　　　　　**Diagram 139-G (Long I-Cut)**

Number 140

Closeout 3's

The careful planning, great execution, great strategy and tactics can all go out the window due to one hustling defender who refuses to give up. In one brief instant the lone hustling defender can take an otherwise open shot and ruin it for a shooter has done everything correctly. For this reason, it is essential 3-point shooters develop the ability to shoot an open shot that has suddenly come under defensive pressure.

Closeout 3's is a drill designed to create sudden defensive pressure. Players are organized in groups of four with three of the players having balls. The first player passes the ball out to the lone 3-point shooter and sprints at the shooter with hands up. The defender secures the rebound and returns to the end of the line. The process continues until the shooter has shot seven shots and then the next shooter replaces the initial shooter (**Diagram 140**).

Once a shot has been deflected or blocked, the shooter now has the option of shot faking and driving one dribble and shooting. This is an excellent drill for teaching decision making and learning to shoot with a rapidly approaching defender. The focus of the shooter should be on the goal and shooting technique. The defender and the possibility of having the shot blocked should not be considered until a defender is able to actually deflect or block a shot.

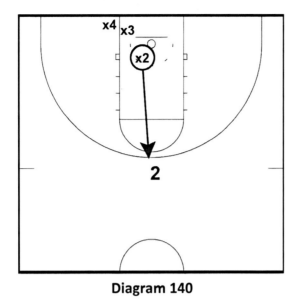

Diagram 140

Fast Break 3-Point Drills

Number 141

2-Man Pitch-a-Heads and Skips

Players are organized into groups at half court based on their fast break position. A three player rush moves up the court. In this instance the pass is pitched-a-head from half court and the 2-man shoots a 3-point shot. This drill must be done at game speed with the next group going as soon as a shot is taken (**Diagram 141-A**).

Two variations of this drill can be easily added. The first is for the 3-man to obtain the offensive rebound of the initial shot, regardless of whether or not the shot was made or missed, and for the 2-man to rotate to the top of the key area for a second 3-point shot attempt.

The second variation is to skip pass the ball from the 2-man to the 3-man for a 3-point shot attempt. This can be a direct skip pass or offensive building blocks such as a penetrate and skip can be used to make the pass (**Diagram 141-B**).

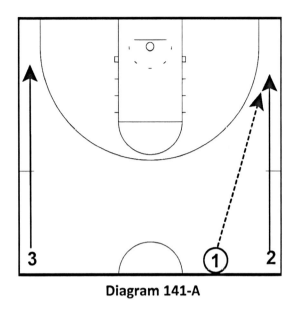

Diagram 141-A

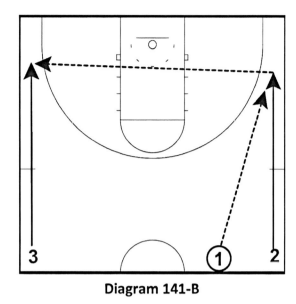

Diagram 141-B

Number 142

3-Man Pitch-a-Heads and Skips

This drill is similar to the one presented in Concept Number 141. The structure of the drill is the same with a cross-court pitch-a-head pass from the point guard or coach being the main difference (**Diagram 142-A**). In Diagram **142-B** a penetrate and skip is depicted as the offensive building block used to create the skip pass.

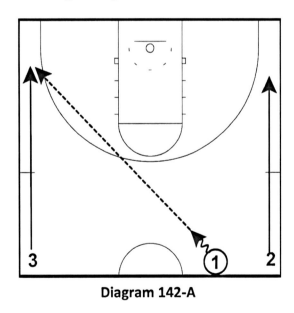

Diagram 142-A

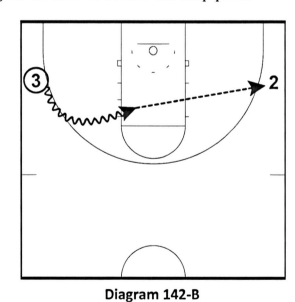

Diagram 142-B

Number 143

1-Man Pull-up 3's

The go to move for a point guard is to penetrate to the goal for a lay-up. This will force the defense to collapse on future penetration allowing the point guard to create scoring opportunities for teammates. The counter move for a point guard is the 3-point shot.

For fast break teams who rely on penetration at the end of their rush up the court, a point guard who can pull up off the dribble and make a 3-point shot will in all likelihood be a devastating penetrator as the defense cannot afford to collapse into the lane to prevent penetration.

The drill is organized as shown in **Diagram 143**. In addition to working on making pull-up 3-point shots, this is an excellent opportunity to work on the inbounds outlet pass to initiate the fast break following a made shot by the opponent. Like the pitch-a-head drills, a variation of this drill can have the point guard rotating to the top of the key for a second 3-point shot attempt regardless of whether or not the first shot is missed.

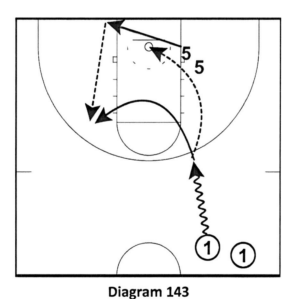

Diagram 143

Number 144

5-Man 3's

The trailer, the 5-man, is nearly always open on the fast break. If a numbered fast break is used and the designated inbounder/trailer is a post player who can shoot the 3-point shot, this is a devastating weapon, forcing the defense into vulnerable alignments early in the offensive possession.

In addition to working on fast break 3-point shooting, this drill incorporates offensive rebounding as well as working on the all-important inbounds pass following a made basket by the opponent (ideally done in under 1.5 seconds).

Diagram 144-A shows the initial alignment with the rebound/inbounds and outlet pass shown in **Diagram 144-B**. By adding a low post player the fanning of the ball out to the trailer for a 3-point attempt can be practiced as well (**Diagram 144-C**).

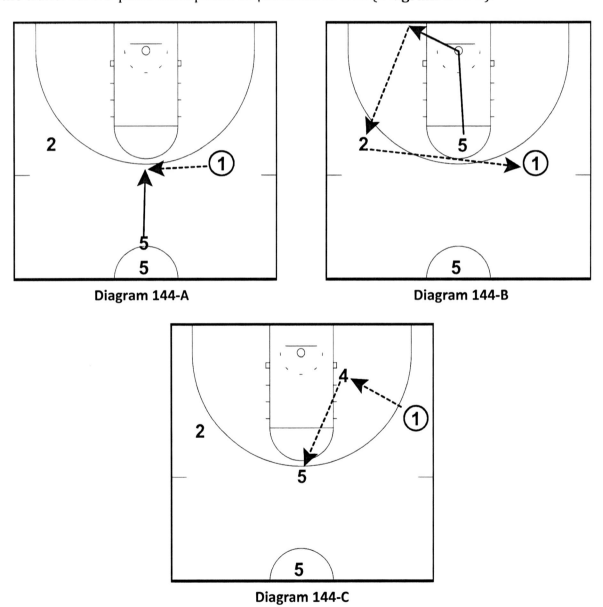

Diagram 144-A   Diagram 144-B

Diagram 144-C

Building Block/Footwork 3's

Number 145

Count the Steps – Triple Attack

In addition to working on the 3-point shot, the focus of this drill is footwork. The so-called "triple cut" is a common cut used in many 3-point plays as well as motion oriented offenses. The shooters start with their inside foot directly under the rim facing the sideline. In the example shown in **Diagram 145-A** the shooter is facing the left sideline.

The shooter makes a tight curl cut, counting steps. The shooter works hard to cut at game speed and take the exact same number of steps each repetition. This helps the shooter to develop good footwork and consistency in the cut and the shot.

In addition to working on the 3-point shot, the counter move of driving against the grain can be practiced as well (**Diagram 145-B**).

A token defender can be added to pressure the cutter to work on decision making as well. If the defender gives the shooter enough space the shooter takes the 3-point shot. If the defender crowds the shooter, the shooter executes a two-inch shot fake and drives against the grain.

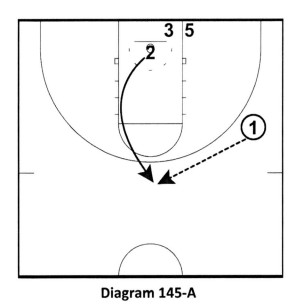

Diagram 145-A

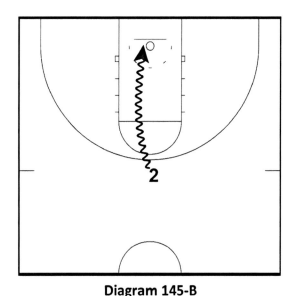

Diagram 145-B

Number 146

Count the Steps – Baseline Dribble Off

This drill uses the same approach as the one described in Concept Number 145. This time the cutter makes a game speed cut to the corner, again counting steps from the foot directly under the goal.

A variation of this drill can include adding the two-inch up fake and driving to the middle for either a lay-up or pull-up jump shot.

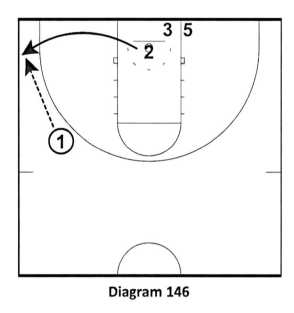

Diagram 146

Number 147

Screening Progression

Successfully shooting of a screen requires good footwork, proper execution of screening and cutting techniques by two players, recognition by every player involved on offense, the ability to communicate with hand signals and finally the ability to shoot off the pass. The screening progression drill is designed to practice all of these essential skills at once.

The drill can be done with or without defense, though in the learning stages it is essential the offense have success and master the small details involved, requiring the defense to be absent from the drill. Defense may be added in stages, starting with token pressure and working up to game intensity.

The drill is a sequenced progression of screens and cuts, hence the name of the drill. The sequence is as follows: down screen, flare screen, back screen, pin screen and re-screen (**Diagrams 147-A** through **147-D**).

The re-screen, setting a particular type of screen followed by the appropriate matching screen, for example, a down screen followed by a flare screen, can be changed each practice session. The cutter shoots each time after coming off the screen taking a total of five shots before rotating to be a passer, screener or rebounder as determined by the coach.

A variation of the drill is to use two passers, passing to the screener reinforcing the concept of being a second cutter. A Shoot-A-Way™ can be used as well to ease the process of running down missed shots and making certain the passers have enough balls to keep the screener and cutter moving at a constant pace.

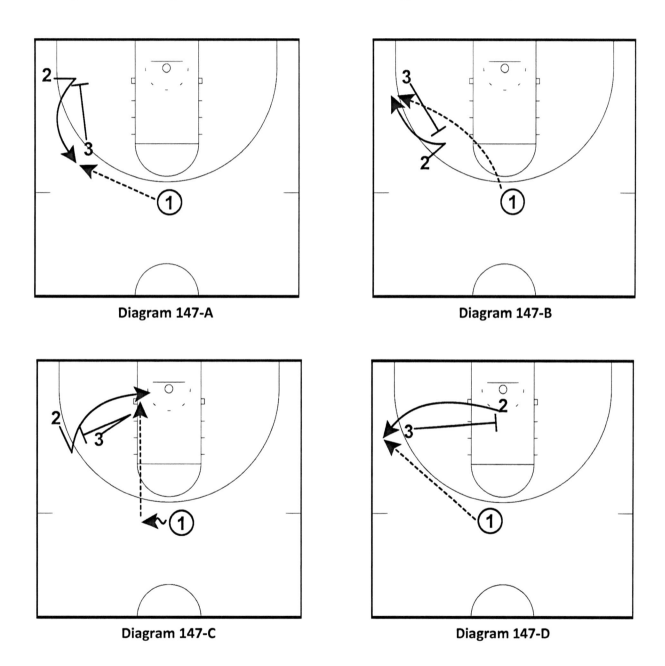

Diagram 147-A   Diagram 147-B

Diagram 147-C   Diagram 147-D

Number 148

Loop 3's

The dribble loop is an effective tactic for use against either zone or man-to-man defense and can be used to enter the ball into the low post or obtain perimeter shots. The drill can be executed from lines of players or if space permits, groups of partners, allowing for a dramatic increase in repetitions. Players execute dribble loops or loop flares. The loop flare can be done with or without a screener setting the flare screen (**Diagrams 148-A** and **148-B**).

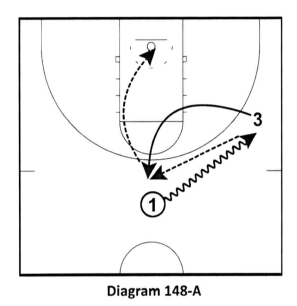
Diagram 148-A

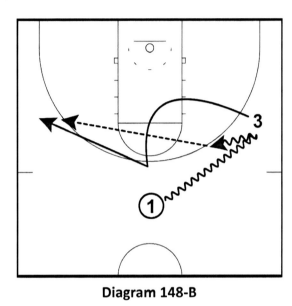
Diagram 148-B

Number 149

32-Point Drill

The 32-Point Drill works on 3-point shooting, the mid-range jump shot and lay-ups. At the conclusion of the drill, the shooter must make two free throws. This drill can take some time so be sure to plan accordingly. There are two simple variations. Scoring for the drill is as follows: 3-point shots are worth three points, the mid-range jump shot is worth two points and the lay-up is worth one point. The two free throws are worth one point each.

The five 3-point shooting spots are utilized. The shooter attempts a 3-point shot, followed by a shot fake, one dribble pull-up 15 ft. jump shot. The third and final shot is a lay-up, utilizing if possible one dribble from the 3-point line. The shooter works from all five of the 3-point shooting spots.

The first, and most time consuming variation of the drill, requires the shooter to score on all three shots at each of the five spots and finish by making two free throws. The total score will be 32 points.

The second, and quicker variation is for the shooter to take only one shot attempt from each shooting spot and shot type. Score is kept by the shooter and totals can be recorded when finished. This can be an excellent competitive shooting drill.

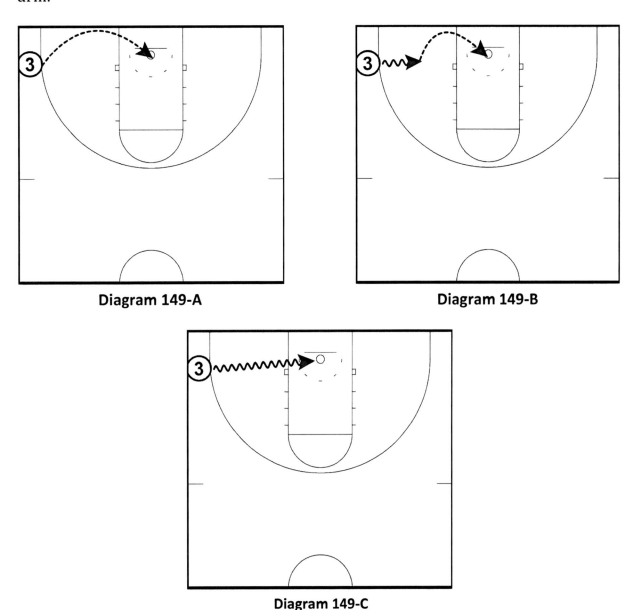

Diagram 149-A   Diagram 149-B

Diagram 149-C

Number 150

Fan the Ball – Two Perimeters and a Post

The objective of this drill is to practice feeding the post and fanning the ball out for 3-point shot attempts, either by passing diagonally opposite or using feed the post and move. The drill can be executed with or without defense. Organization can be done in lines or using groups of three at every goal if space and facilities permit. **Diagrams 150-B** and **150-B** depict how the drill should be executed.

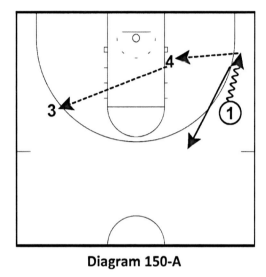

Diagram 150-A

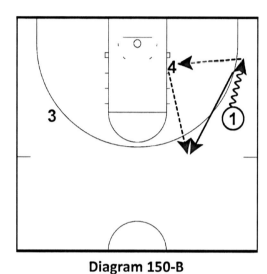

Diagram 150-B

21

Secondary Breaks for the 3-Point Shot

Zone Secondary

Some teams as part of their game strategy to deal with effective fast breaking teams will play a zone defense so the defenders can make defensive transition rapidly and then move smoothly into a zone defense, hoping to be set and organized faster than if playing man-to-man defense. Given that many teams attack zones with more patience than man-to-man offenses, the mere presence of a zone defense can slow down teams that otherwise play at a fast tempo.

To combat this strategy, it is necessary to be able to attack zone defenses with the same speed and organization as attacking man-to-man defense. The zone secondary shown here is particularly effective against aggressive zones that tend to match-up man-to-man with offensive players in the zone defender's "zone" or "area."

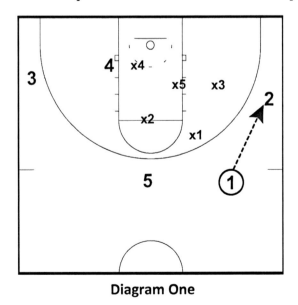

Diagram One

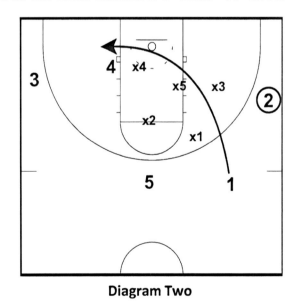

Diagram Two

The entry to Zone Secondary is shown in **Diagram One** and **Diagram Two**. After passing to #2, #1 makes a basket cut and clears to the other side of the court. Depending on the 3 pt. shooting ability of the two players, it may be desirable for #2 to be the first cutter if #1 is the better 3 pt. shooter.

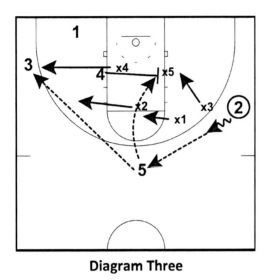

Diagram Three

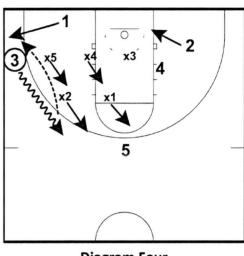

Diagram Four

Diagram Three depicts the ball reversal action and the movement of the zone defenders in reaction to the ball movement. Note the screening and posting action of #4 setting up a possible high low pass. **Diagram Four** depicts the first dribble off and resulting defensive adjustments as well as the pass back to #1.

In **Diagram 5** when #3 dribbles off the baseline, the rear defender of the zone defense will follow #3, pressuring the ball, as #3 dribbles off the baseline. #1 moves from the short post to the corner on the baseline. #2 fills the short post. #4 flashes into the high post area to occupy the zone defenders in that area. #5 moves to the opposite side of the court to balance the floor. #3 must drive into the area of the offensive court forcing zone defenders to "bump" from a backline defender to a frontline defender.

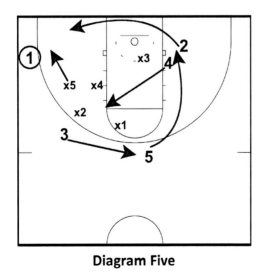

Diagram Five

Diagram Six

Diagram Six depicts the use of the short post option with #1 passing the ball to #2 in the short post. #3 finds the seam in the defense diagonal and opposite of the ball while #4 and #5 step to openings in the interior of the defense looking for passes for post scoring opportunities.

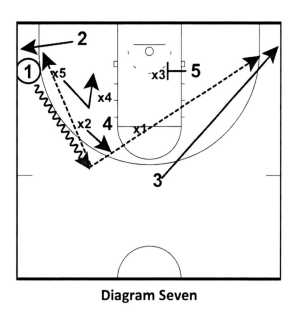

Diagram Seven

Diagram Seven depicts the second and final baseline dribble off. #3 cuts behind #5 for a screen-in opportunity and #2 fills the ball side corner for a 3-point shot opportunity. #1 reads the zone defense and takes advantage of the best opportunity or makes the decision to enter zone attack offense.

Zone Special

The Zone Special secondary break takes advantage of the Olivet approach of running the low post the opposite side of the court from the ball, creating space on the ball side. After passing to #2 the point guard cuts to the ball side short post (**Diagram One**). The quick entry pass into the short post can result in an inside scoring opportunity (**Diagram Two**).

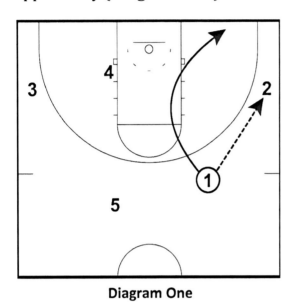

Diagram One

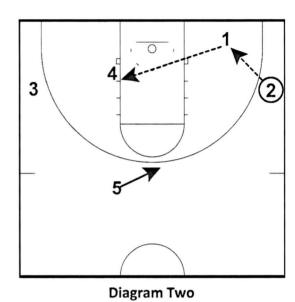

Diagram Two

If the inside scoring opportunity is not available, the remaining perimeter players immediately seek seams in the zone defense looking for a pass from the short post area (**Diagram Three**) following which #1 cuts to the corner opposite the short post. **Diagram Four** depicts a screen-in opportunity as #5 cuts inside.

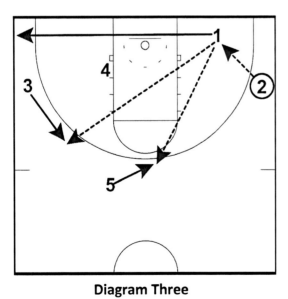

Diagram Three

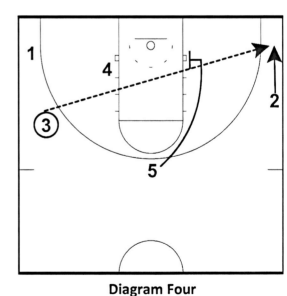

Diagram Four

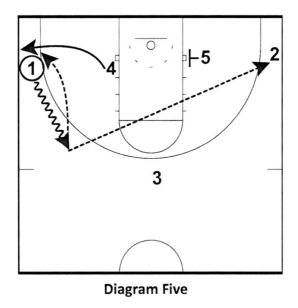

Diagram Five

Diagram Five depicts a dribble off by #1 with the option of a skip pass to #2 on the screen-in or a 3-point shot by #4 (if the post player is capable of hitting this shot).

Triple

Triple is a man-to-man secondary break that takes advantage of screening action and several offensive building blocks such as driving against the grain or fanning the ball from the post. **Diagram One** depicts the initial alignment. Diagram Two depicts the initial screening and cutting action. #1 has the option of feeding the post or hitting #2 coming off the triple screen action.

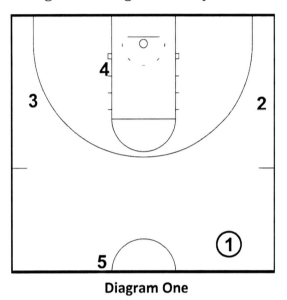

Diagram One

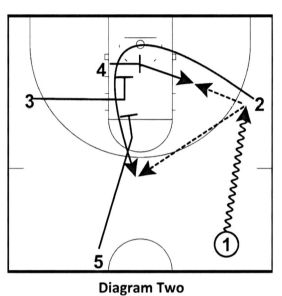

Diagram Two

Diagram Three depicts the spacing following the screening action. In this example #2 has decided to drive against the grain for a lay-up instead of taking a 3-point shot. This action sets up penetrate and pitch as well as a Euro with #1. **Diagram Four** shows the low post fanning the ball to the perimeter players.

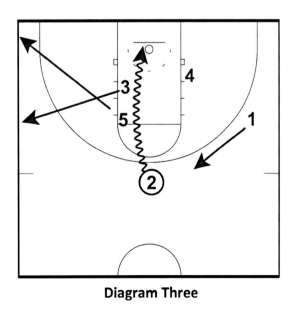

Diagram Three

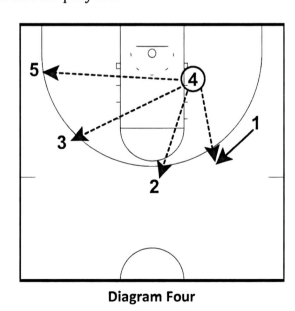

Diagram Four

Fade

Fade is an adaptation to Triple when the defense "cheats" by running a defender to the top of the key rather than fighting through the screens when #2 makes the cut over the three screens. **Diagram One** depicts the initial alignment.

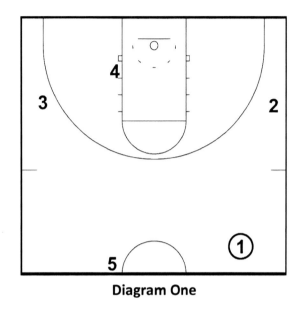
Diagram One

The adjustments to Triple are shown in **Diagram Two**. Rather than setting down screens, #3 and #5 set a wall screen on the cheating defender who simply avoids the screens in Triple and cuts to the top of the key. #2 adjusts his/her cut by fading behind the wall screen. #1 must reverse direction and make a skip pass for the 3-point attempt.

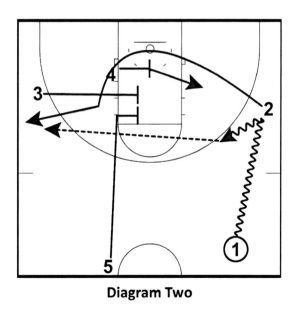
Diagram Two

Double Stagger

Double Stagger takes advantage of perimeter players who possess good 3-point shooting skills and the ability to penetrate. **Diagram One** depicts the initial alignment and the entry pass off the fast break.

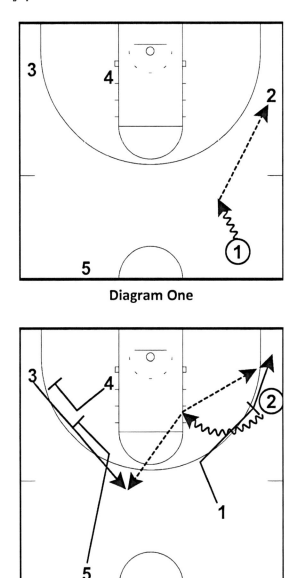

Diagram One

Diagram Two

Diagram Two depicts the screening and cutting action of Double Stagger. #4 and #5 set a double staggered screen for #3 while #1 sets a ball screen for #2 who drives the middle. #2 can drive for a lay-up or hit #1 or #3 for a 3-point opportunity.

22

Set Plays (Quick Hitters) for the 3-Point Shot

The following five set plays, or quick hitters, are designed to obtain a wide range of scoring options, including 2-point field goals. All five are run from a 1-4 high set to cause the defense to align in positions preventing the establishment of help side defense if run against a man-to-man defense or to shift the zone defense prior to the commencement of the running of the play. As shown, the plays are to be run against man-to-man defense. With adjustments all except "Maui" can be run effectively against a zone defense. Adapt the plays to your personnel and personality as a coach or use them as a starting point to devise your own quick hitters.

Denver

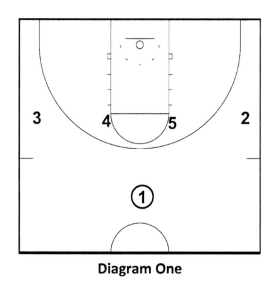

Diagram One

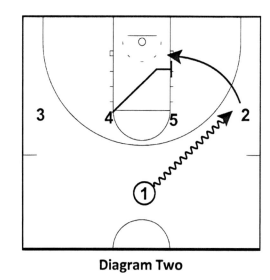

Diagram Two

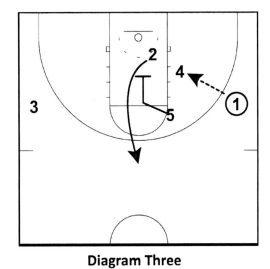

Diagram Three

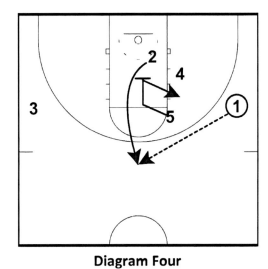

Diagram Four

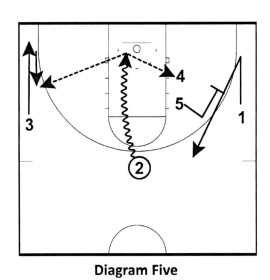

Diagram Five

Dribble Over

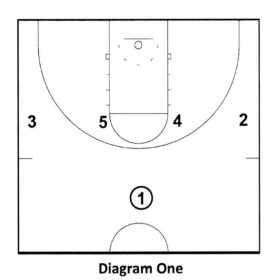

Diagram One

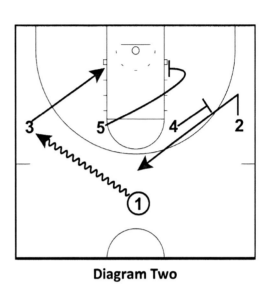

Diagram Two

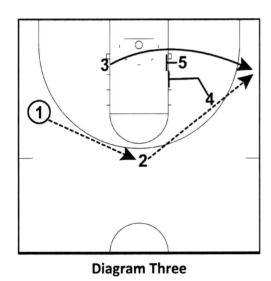

Diagram Three

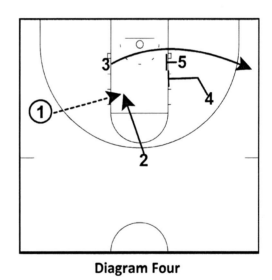

Diagram Four

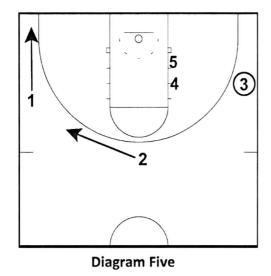

Diagram Five

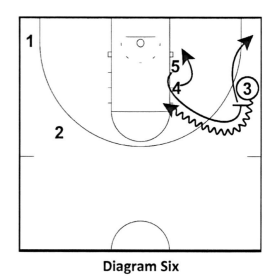

Diagram Six

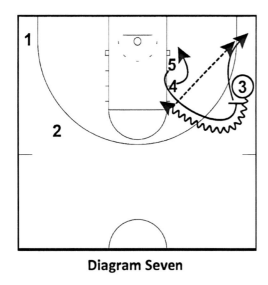

Diagram Seven

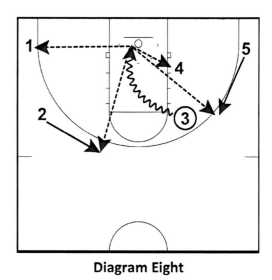

Diagram Eight

Post Option

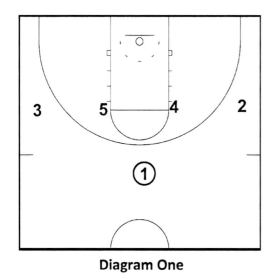

Diagram One

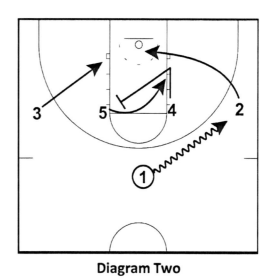

Diagram Two

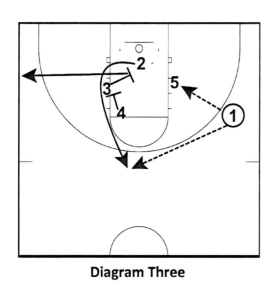

Diagram Three

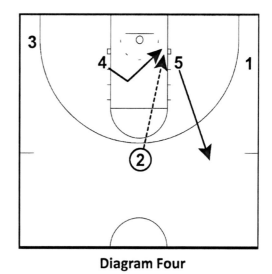

Diagram Four

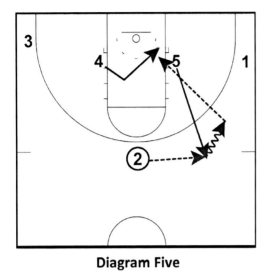

Diagram Five

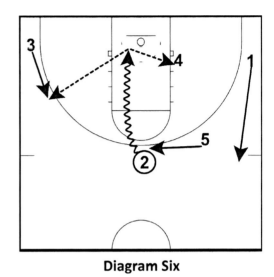

Diagram Six

Maui

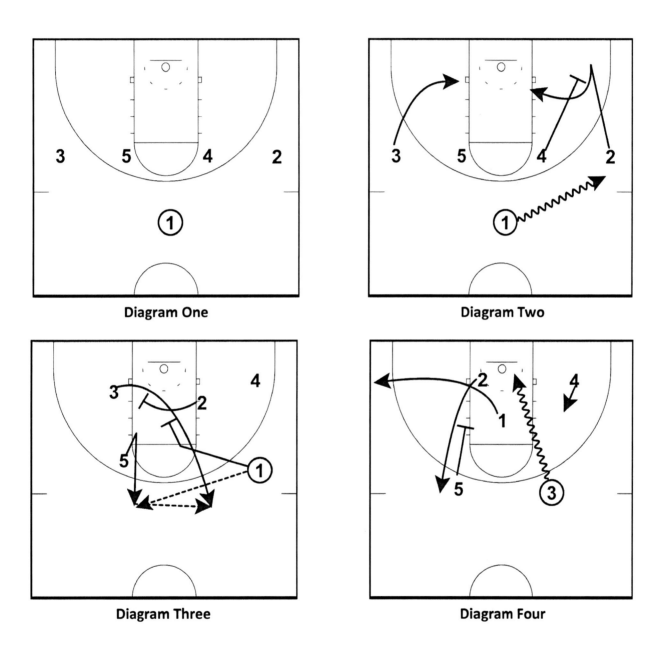

Diagram One

Diagram Two

Diagram Three

Diagram Four

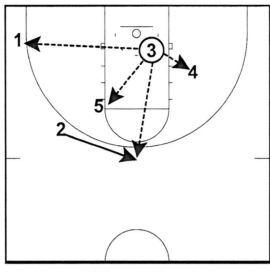

Diagram Five

Duke

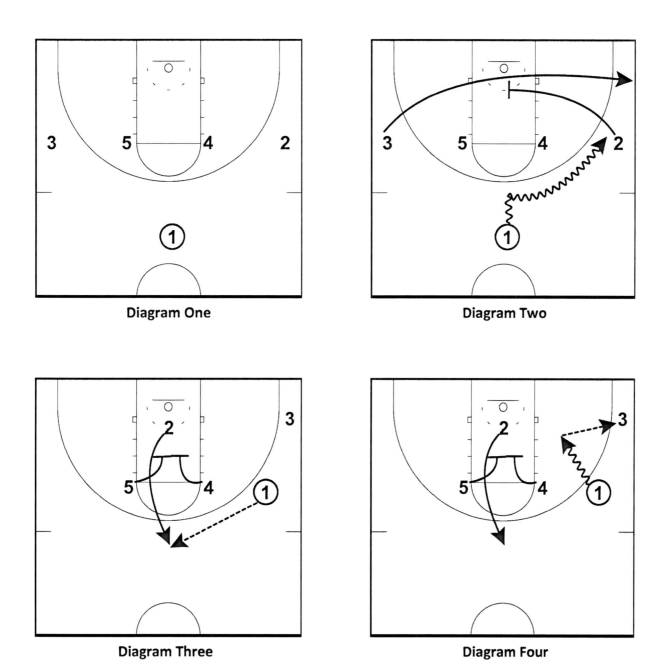

Diagram One

Diagram Two

Diagram Three

Diagram Four

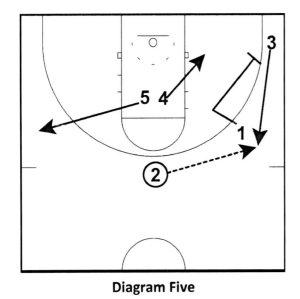

Diagram Five

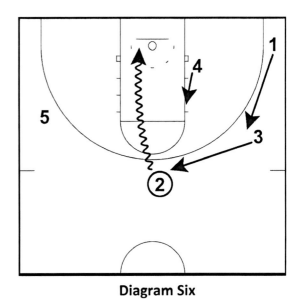

Diagram Six

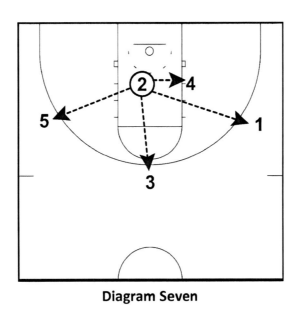

Diagram Seven

23

Baseline Out-of-Bounds Plays for the 3-Point Shot

Double Dribble Off versus a Zone Defense

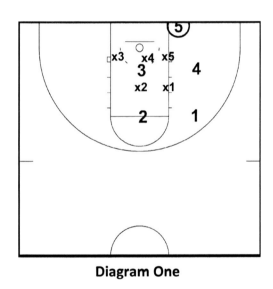

Diagram One

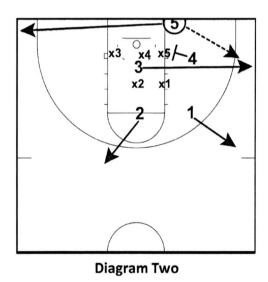

Diagram Two

Double Dribble Off is meant to be used against a zone defense. It can be a slow to develop play requiring 5-7 seconds of time in order to be effective. **Diagram One** depicts the initial alignment against a 2-3 zone defense. **Diagram Two** depicts the initial cutting and screening action.

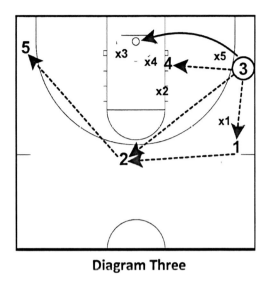

Diagram Three

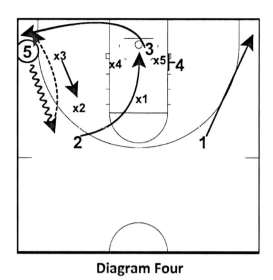

Diagram Four

Diagram Three depicts the options available to reverse the ball quickly or enter the ball into the low post for a quick inside score. **Diagram Four** depicts the beginning of the dribble off action. The objective of this tactic is to force the zone defender X3 to cover the same open area quickly two or three times. Note #1 has drifted to the opposite corner and is using a screen-in being set by the lost post player #4 to set up a 3-point attempt.

Diagram Five

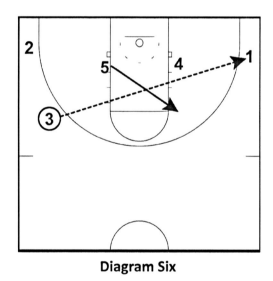

Diagram Six

The second dribble off action is depicted in **Diagram Five**. Note #5 cuts into the ball side low post for a possible post feed. In **Diagram Six** #3 has decided to use the screen-in option and make a skip pass to #1 for the 3-point shot. The defenders have been omitted for clarity in **Diagrams Six** and **Seven.**

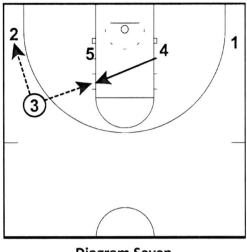

Diagram Seven

In this diagram #3 has decided to take advantage of a slow moving baseline defender and pass the ball back to #2 for a 3-point shot. Another option is depicted as well as #3 enters the ball into the high post to the flash cutter #4.

Option

The play "Option" is so named due to the various options available for scoring. **Diagram One** depicts the initial alignment and the initial cuts are shown in **Diagram Two.**

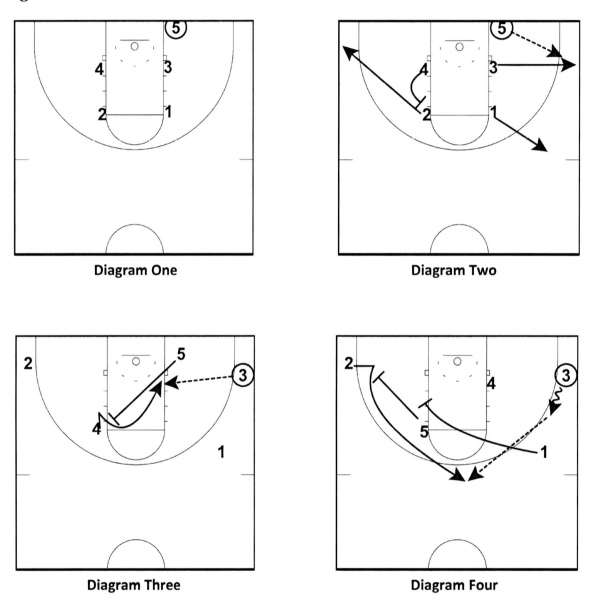

Diagram One   Diagram Two

Diagram Three   Diagram Four

Diagram Three shows the post option with #5 setting a screen for #4 in the high post opposite the ball. **Diagram Four** shows the double staggered screen away from the ball set by #5 and #1 for #2.

Diagram Five

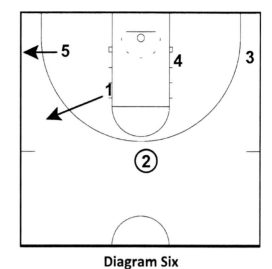

Diagram Six

If the ball has been passed into the low post of the post to post screen, the double staggered screen is still set as the post, #4, may fan the ball out to #2 (**Diagram Five**). **Diagrams Six** and **Seven** depict the conclusion of the play with the spacing of the screeners and #3 and the penetration of #2 if a 3-point shot is not available off the double staggered screen.

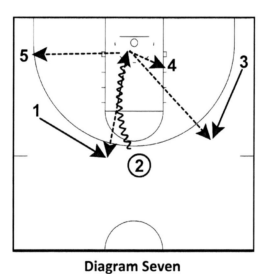

Diagram Seven

Two

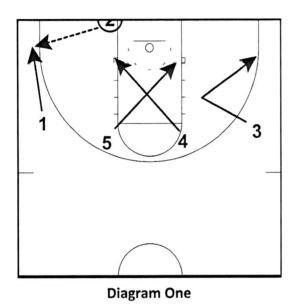

Diagram One

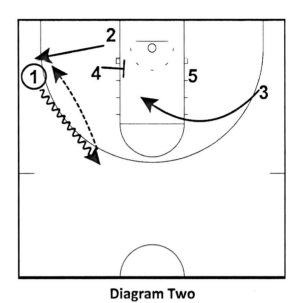

Diagram Two

Two is a simple play designed to attack a zone defense. The initial cuts to get open do not require a pass to #1 (**Diagram One**). With four cutters cutting to the ball, the zone defense will be able to only cover three of the four cutters. Most teams will protect the rim and cover the two interior cutters and the opposite wing, #3 can be difficult to pass to. If the ball is passed to one of the interior cutters, a quick 2-point post shot is taken.

If the ball is passed to one of the wings in either corner, the play is executed as shown in **Diagram Two** on the side of the floor the ball has been passed to. The ball side low post sets a screen-in against the zone defender as the ball is dribbled off the baseline. The inbounder cuts in behind the dribble off while the opposite wing flashes into the middle to form a rebound triangle. The inbounder will almost always have a 3-point shot available. #1 will get back for defensive floor balance after passing the ball to the inbounder.

Box Three

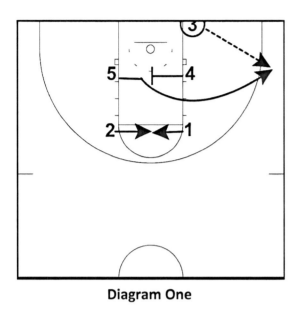

Diagram One

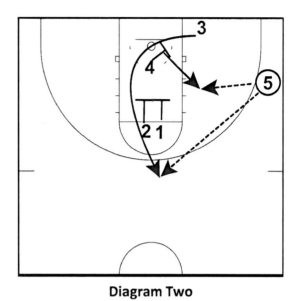

Diagram Two

Box Three can be run against a zone or man-to-man defense. This simple play can produce a quick low post score as the post screener becomes the second cutter or a 3-point shot as #3 comes of the wall screen set in the foul line area.

24

Sideline Out-of-Bounds Plays for the 3-Point Shot

High Low

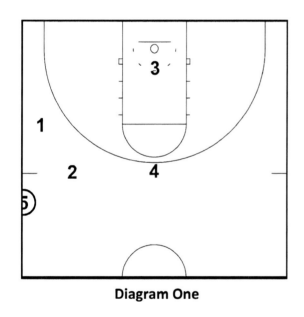

Diagram One

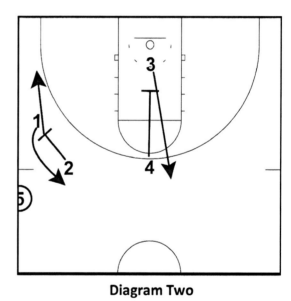

Diagram Two

High low can be run successfully against both man-to-man and zone defenses. As depicted in the diagrams the play is being executed against man-to-man defense. To adjust for zone defense, it will be necessary to have an idea in advance of what zone the opponent will be playing and how the zone will cover specific options. The adjustments will be in where the screens take place and where the post player seals for the post-up option. **Diagram One** depicts the initial alignment while **Diagram Two** depicts the initial screening and cutting action. Players #2 and #3 both potentially may be open for 3-point shots on the inbounds pass.

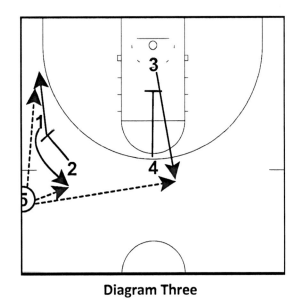

Diagram Three

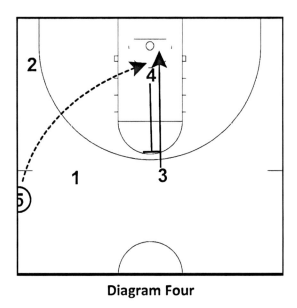

Diagram Four

Diagram Three depicts all of the inbounds passing options. If your team is fortunate enough to have a forward who is an excellent leaper **Diagram Four** depicts an excellent option for a 2-point shot, particularly if only one or two seconds remain. If a zone defense is being utilized, #4 must be told exactly which defender to screen and at what angle.

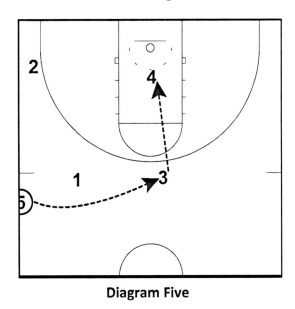

Diagram Five

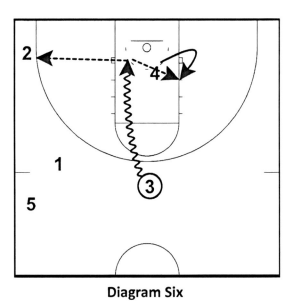

Diagram Six

Diagram Five depicts the high low action with #4 isolated in the lane. **Diagram Six** depicts the penetrate and pitch action against a man-to-man defense. #2 spots up in the corner and #4 moves out of the lane to create room for a passing angle while at the same time turning to face the basket and preparing to shoot upon catching the ball.

JP

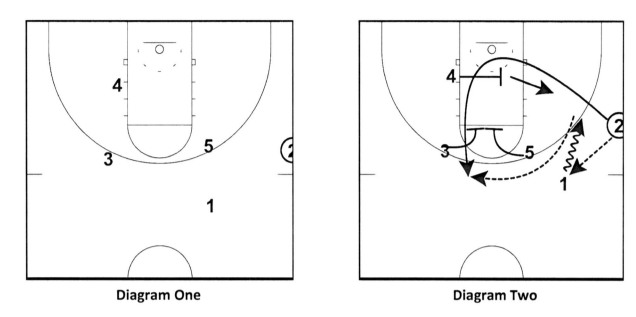

| Diagram One | Diagram Two |

JP can be run against man-to-man or zone defenses. The adjustments consist of timing and the exact location of where the double screen will be set. **Diagram One** shows the initial alignment. **Diagram Two** depicts the execution of the play itself.

Lob 3

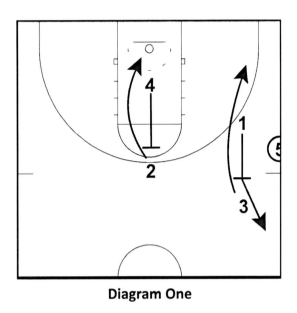

Diagram One

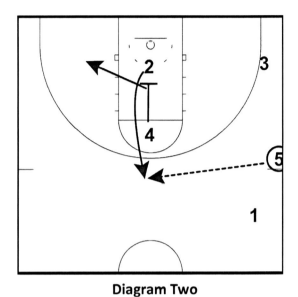

Diagram Two

Lob is best utilized against an aggressive denial type of man-to-man defense. A lob pass for a 2-point shot can be obtained on the inbounds pass if the back screen set by #4 for #2 is successful as shown in **Diagram One**. Diagram Two depicts the first 3-point shot option with the inbounds pass to #2 following the second screen from #4. **Diagram Three** depicts the penetration by #2 creating a pass to #4 for a 2-point shot or the "Euro" option to #3.

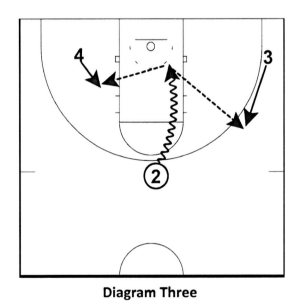

Diagram Three

Cut

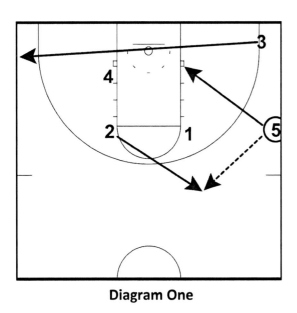

Diagram One

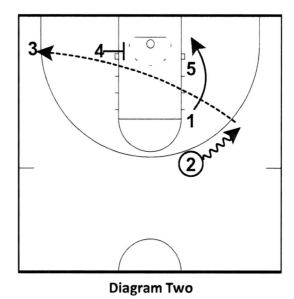

Diagram Two

Cut is meant to be run against a 2-3 zone defense and makes use of two zone attack offensive building blocks, the dribble off and the screen in. **Diagram One** depicts the initial alignment, cuts and inbounds pass. **Diagram Two** depicts the first screen-in while **Diagram Three** depicts the dribble off and second screen-in.

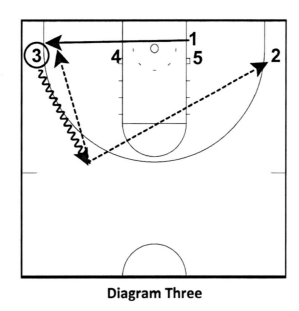

Diagram Three

Wolf

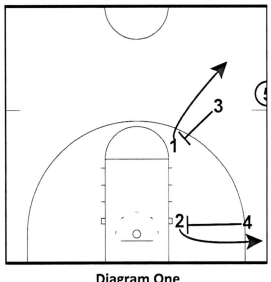

Diagram One

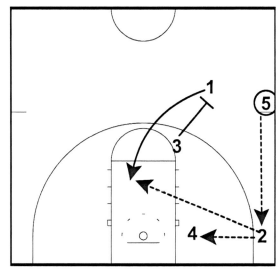

Diagram Two

Wolf can be used against man-to-man and zone defenses for the initial quick 3-point shot. **Diagrams One** and **Two** depict the initial alignment and cutting action. #2 is the player who will have the open 3-point shot on the inbounds pass if the defense is effectively screened. Against man-to-man defense #4 will be completely isolated in the low post as well for an excellent 2-point opportunity. **Diagram Three** depicts the final 3-point shot opportunity against man-to-man as #1 drives creating a "Euro" opportunity for #3. This option is nearly always available against man-to-man defenses.

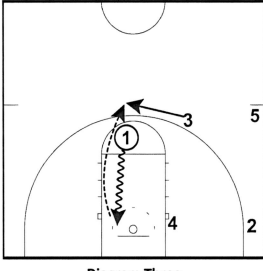

Diagram Three

25

Creating an Individual Workout Program for 3-Point Shooting

Simply providing one standard workout for developing 3-point shooters would be counterproductive and against my approach to coaching and sharing information with other coaches. Every program and every player is different. Different approaches may be required to fit the program and the player. In fact, over the course of the many years spent in developing shooters, my approach to developmental workouts changed depending on the players available and the needs of the team for the coming season.

The first considerations in planning a workout program are developing individual shooting technique followed by shooting volume. How will players be guided in the process of developing shooting technique? How many shots do the players need to take in the off-season, pre-season and in-season?

Range Testing

The first step in the entire process should be an accurate range test. This will help the player and coach identify with a degree of accuracy the actual shooting range of the player and any identifiable flaws or tendencies in the player's shot.

Rules of Range Testing

Every player in the program should be range tested and a record of the results kept. This is a valuable tool for identifying areas of needed improvement, the actual range a player can shoot from with a degree of reliability and objective measure to be used to convince both the player and parent of what the player's actual shooting range and ability is.

The range test is a valuable motivational tool in the process of developing shooting ability. Players have an easily identifiable standard of achievement and a clear idea of what to work on in order to improve and be "green lighted" for an increased shooting range.

Players are not allowed to shoot beyond their established range in games and scrimmage situations unless specifically instructed to do so.

Players are allowed to shoot beyond their established range during shooting drills when instructed to do so in order to develop the range of their shot.

Players may re-test at designated times during the course of the season. Any player who is able to improve his or her range test score is then "green lighted" to shoot from the improved distance.

Range Testing Procedure

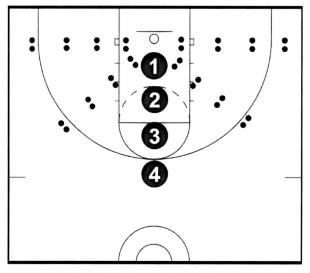

Sample Range Test Chart

The range test chart shown is a sample. The numbered circles are shown in lieu of the paired dots to show distance. The first circle is 6-8 feet, the second circle as at 10-12 feet, the third at 15 feet and the fourth and final just beyond the 3-point line. Again, the range test chart shown is just a sample. The distances can be made shorter and more "layers" added to the test.

Once a range test has been decided upon, make a master range test chart and duplicate as many copies as needed. Be sure to add a chart to record the final field goal percentages the player achieved at each distance.

The test starts on the right side of the goal with the player taking two shots from each pair of dots. The player shoots all ten shots at that distance, moving in a semi-circle around the goal before moving back to the next distance in the test. If a player makes a shot, circle the dot. If the player misses the shot, record the miss as long, short, left or right by making a tiny hash mark indicating how the shot was missed. This information can be invaluable in analyzing possible flaws in the player's shot. For example, if the majority of hash indicators are on the top of the dot and slanted to the right, it is an indication the player misses long and to the right. Feedback can then be given to the player on how to correct the flaw in the shot.

In addition to learning of consistent flaws in a shooter's technique, it is also possible to determine where on the court the player is the most effective. If the player misses on consistently on the left side of the court but makes 70% or 80% of the shot attempts on the right, the coach now knows to run sets for that player on the right side of the court.

For a player to "pass" a distance in the range test, the player must make 60% of the shot attempts at that distance. Why 60%? The player is not tired, not being defended, is shooting under optimal shooting conditions and game slippage has to be allowed for.

Keep Records

Always keep copies of the player's range test results. This is a valuable source of information that can serve as a record of improvement or sadly, proof positive of a player's limitations in a parent coach meeting.

Know Your Players

The information gained in the range test can be invaluable for a coach when planning offense, inbounds plays, last second shot sets and player roles.

Key Considerations for Planning an Individual Workout Program

As stated earlier, every program is different and will have different requirements and challenges that will need to be considered when planning the Individual Workout Program (IWP). The factors to consider include:

- Availability of gym time or goals for players to shoot at
- State, district or conference rules concerning off-season work
- Commitment level of players
- Time available of the players to perform the IWP
- Number of days per week
- Repetition with variety
- Teaching time

Items to include in the workout regardless of the level of difficulty or amount shots to be taken:

- Warm-up the body
- Warm-up ball handling
- Warm-up the shot (shooting progression)
- Form repetitions
- Free throws

- Off the dribble
- Off the pass
- Special situation
- Variations
- Put-backs

Form a Pattern for the IWP

Players need to warm-up their body, ball handling and shot and this is how every workout should start. The next phase should be some form of a shooting progression (more later) followed by form repetitions of the 3-point shot for a high volume of shots before moving on to specific types of 3-point shooting. Each type of 3-point shooting should be interspersed with 10 free throw makes, not attempts.

Remember, players need repetition with variety. Each workout needs to be both similar and with high repetitions, but have variety in some way. My recommendation is to work on specific 3-point skills or situations on different days of the week. For example, work on the footwork of a specific cut followed by catching the ball in a specific spot and shooting the 3-point shot.

Shooting Progression

Pitchers would never walk out to the pitching mound and start a game without first warming up their arm. Yet basketball players consistently do the basketball equivalent of not warming up their arm before throwing, they will start shooting 3-point shots without warming up their shot.

Coaches will want to have players focus on different items in a warm-up shooting progression. My list includes the following:

- Green light shooting (swish with perfect from 20 shots from 3 feet).
- Shadow shooting to check form
- Grooving the shot from three feet to behind the 3-point line. If the shooter swishes the shot, the shooter can take a normal step back. If the shooter draws iron, the shooter takes the shot again from the same spot. If the shooter misses, the shooter must take a step forward.

Shot Clubs

I like the idea of shooting clubs. A general shooting program is designed for all players. It is flexible enough in the parts where volume of shots taken that players can take more shots if they so desire. Players must keep track of their workouts and record the number of 3-point shots they make. Using a pre-determined start and end date, players can earn membership in 1,000, 2,000 or 5,000 3-point shots made clubs. T-shirts can be awarded for the level of club the player earns membership in. This approach allows a coach to establish a reasonable minimum amount of off-season work yet allows players with a higher level of commitment to display it to their teammates. Over time, this approach can gradually raise the level of commitment in the entire program. Records should be kept and posted each season to show what has been accomplished in the past. There will be a demonstrable correlation between the work done in the off-season and the success of the team in the following season.

Be Creative In Designing Your Own IWPs

It is your program. You know what is needed better than any other individual. Be creative in designing an approach that is realistic, goal oriented, has repetition with variety, meets the specific needs of the program for the coming season, develops players and can have some fun built into it.

Communicate with other programs successful at developing 3-point shooters and find out what those programs are doing. Borrow ideas from the IWPs those coaches have developed and incorporate them into the workouts designed for your program.

26

Twelve Ways to Defend the 3-Point Shot

Free throws and lay-ups are how basketball games are won. However, as an advocate of the 3-point shot, I believe the "3" can and will keep a team in games and is a great equalizer for teams who are not as big or athletic but who can shoot the ball with accuracy.

Great 3-point shooters can keep a team in a game and on those special nights, upset an opponent seemingly single-handedly, making it essential to teach your team how to successfully defend either one great 3-point shooter or defend a team of solid 3-point shooters.

Here are 12 rules or concepts for defending the 3-point shot:

1) Identify the 3-point shooter(s). You have to know who they are in order to defend them.

2) Play no help defense. Assign your best defensive player to the great 3-point shooter and do not give help with that defender, eliminating many of the easy and quick ways to set up a 3-point shooter. Penetration is one of the easiest set-ups for a 3-point shot and not helping takes that option away. In effect, the defense is playing a box and one.

3) Closeout with high hands. A defender should always "think shot and play drive" and have high hands when closing out on any offensive player in order to prevent a clean look at the rim. This is particularly important with a 3-point shooter.

4) Deny the 3-point shooter when playing pack-line man-to-man. Most pack type defenses do not contest any non-penetrating pass made beyond the 3-point line. Denying the pass to the 3-point shooter and playing regular defense on all other offensive players is disruptive and effective.

5) Be aware of long rebounds. Long rebounds allow for easier offensive rebounds for 3-point shooters. Statistically, a 3-point shooter who is able to obtain the ball for a second shot from the inside out shoots at a much higher percentage than normal.

6) Shade in a zone defense. Know where the 3-point shooter is and shade towards the shooter.

7) Make the 3-point shooter put the ball on the floor. Not only does this make the shooter less effective, the shooter will drive inside the 3-point arc, eliminating the threat of a 3-point goal.

8) When screened leave no gap on the catch. It is not always possible to prevent a 3-point shooter from catching the ball, particularly after a screen. Arrive the same time the ball does and leave no gap, forcing the shooter to drive.

9) Pick up and deny at the NBA 3-point line. Locate the 3-point shooter by half court while in defensive transition and deny the shooter from the NBA 3-point line.
10) Late in the game, to protect a lead, force the 3-point shooter to go backdoor. This eliminates the threat of a 3-point shot.

11) Late in the game, to protect a lead when up by four, foul. If the opponent is not in the bonus, they will have to inbounds the ball, reducing their opportunity for scoring. If the opponent is in the 1-and-1 bonus, the opponent has to make the first free throw, miss the second and obtain the rebound and pass the ball out to a 3-point shooter for a 3-point shot to score three points, tying the game. The same situation applies in the double bonus.

12) Trap the great shooter. If your team plays a trapping defense out of its man-to-man, this can be an extraordinary tactic. Trap only the great 3-point shooter, forcing the shooter to give the ball up.

For these tactics to be effective, they must be practiced regularly and be a part of your normal defensive arsenal.

27

There is Always More to Learn

Suggested Viewing

DVD – *DVD 3 – Half-Court 'Attack' Offense* by Doug Porter
Available from *Roundball Productions* http://roundball.net/

DVD – *The Century Scoring System* by Doug Porter
Available from Championship Productions

DVD - *DVD 9 Utilizing and Defending the 3-Point Shot* by Don Meyer
Available direct from Coach Meyer at
www.northern.edu/Coach_Meyer/educational_dvd.aspx

DVD - *DVD 15 Drills for Teaching Individual Fundamentals and Team Offense* by **Don Meyer**
Available direct from Coach Meyer at
www.northern.edu/Coach_Meyer/educational_dvd.aspx

DVD - *DVD 19 Drills and Techniques To Improve Your Shooting* **by Don Meyer**
Available direct from Coach Meyer at
www.northern.edu/Coach_Meyer/educational_dvd.aspx

DVD – *3-Point Shooting Made Easy* by Dick Baumgartner
Available direct from http://dickbshootingcamp.com/

DVD - *The Don Eddy Skill System of Shooting* by Don Eddy
Available direct from http://www.debb.com/

Suggested Reading

You Haven't Taught Until They Have Learned: John Wooden's Teaching Principles and Practices by Sven Nater

Wooden: A Lifetime of Observations and Reflections On and Off the Court by Coach John Wooden and Steve Jamison

Practical Modern Basketball by Coach John Wooden

Coaching the System by Doug Porter

Basketball Skills and Drills by Jerry Krause

Becoming a Great Shooter by Don Meyer

Offensive Perimeter Play by Don Meyer

Basketball Fundamental Drills by Don Meyer

Don Meyer's Basketball Coaching Academy Notes by Don Meyer

Game Strategy and Tactics for Basketball: Bench Coaching for Success by Kevin Sivils

The Game of Basketball: Basketball Fundamentals, Intangibles and Finer Points of the Game for Coaches, Players and Fans by Kevin Sivils

Better Basketball Practices by Kevin Sivils

28

Final Thoughts

Great 3-point shooting teams are made not born. I am convinced of this based on experience. Simply wishing for a team made up of great 3-point shooters won't make it happen.

All of the ideas and information presented in this book are of no value without the players who can make these concepts come to life. To put it bluntly, you have to have players who can shoot the 3-point shot.

This requires daily practice time committed to both shooting 3-point shots as well as perfecting the footwork, passing and catching skills and the ability to execute the offensive building blocks used to create 3-point shot opportunities.

The off-season is the time where great 3-point shooting teams are really made. It takes time, effort, commitment and persistence on the part of both the shooter and the coach to develop a player into a sound and consistent shooter who can be relied upon to make 3-point shots night after night under the pressure of game competition.

Wishing for it to happen won't work. Spending a few minutes a day in practice won't work either. If you want your teams to be deadly from behind the 3-point line, you will have to make the commitment as a coach to make it happen. This means not only a emphasis on the 3-point shot, but the actual commitment of time to developing the skills and knowledge.

The 3-point shot can be a great equalizer for teams who lack size and athleticism. It can take teams who possess size and athletic ability to the next level, serving as the skill that separates this team from being one of the good teams to a great one.

But it takes commitment for it to happen and the commitment has to start with the coach. Master the ideas and skills needed to teach your players and your team who to utilize the 3-point shot. Make the commitment to display the patience needed for your players and your team to develop their skills. Finally, discipline your self to stay the course and stick to the program of development. You will not regret it.

29

About the Author

A 25 year veteran of the coaching profession, with twenty-two of those years spent as a varsity head coach, Coach Kevin Sivils amassed 464 wins and his TEAMs earned berths in the state play-offs 19 out of 22 seasons with his TEAMs advancing to the state semi-finals three times. An eight time Coach of the Year Award winner, Coach Sivils has traveled as far as the Central African Republic to conduct coaching clinics. Coach Sivils first coaching stint was as an assistant coach for his college alma mater, Greenville College, located in Greenville, Illinois.

Coach Sivils holds a BA with a major in physical education and a minor in social studies from Greenville College and a MS in Kinesiology with a specialization in Sport Psychology from Louisiana State University. He also holds a Sport Management certification from the United States Sports Academy.

In addition to being a basketball coach, Coach Sivils is a classroom instructor and has taught U.S. Government, U.S. History, the History of WW II, and Physical Education and has won awards for
excellence in teaching and Teacher of the Year. He has served as an Athletic Director and Assistant Athletic Director and has also been involved in numerous professional athletic organizations.

Sivils is married to the former Lisa Green of Jackson, Michigan, and the happy couple are the proud parents of three children, Danny, Katie, and Emily. Rounding out the Sivils family are three dogs, Angel, Berkeley, and Alec. A native of Louisiana, Coach Sivils currently resides in the Great State of Texas.

30

To Contact the Author

If you have any questions about the content of *Fine Tuning Your 3-Point Offense* or any of my other books, please feel free to contact me! I can be contacted by e-mail at:

info@kcsbasketball.com

To sign-up for my FREE e-Newsletter, *The Roundball Report*, please visit my website CoachSivils.com and register for the newsletter.

Website

To visit my website please go to www.CoachSivils.com or www.kcsbasketball.com

Blogs

To visit my blog about basketball, *The Basketball Coach's Notebook*, go to http://www.kcsbasketball.com/blog/

To visit my blog about the mental side of sports, *Teach to Win*!, go to www.teachtowin.com

Twitter

To follow on Twitter please go to *https://twitter.com/#!/CoachSivils*

Facebook

To follow on Facebook please go to *http://www.facebook.com/CoachSivils?sk=wall*

Please be sure to "Like" the page!

Amazon Store

Please visit the Amazon Store at CoachSivils.com.

31

Lagniappe – Something Extra

Go To and Counter Moves – Concept Number 96

The following is a list of moves and counter moves that players should develop in pairs.

Dribble Moves

Go to move:
Crossover dribble
Crossover dribble with hesitation
Pullback crossover-dribble

Counter move:
In-out dribble
Hesitation-accelerate
Pullback and go

Post moves

Go to move:
Baseline drop step
Turn and shoot
Mid-lane drop step

Counter move:
Jump hook to the middle
McHale move (up and under)
Catch and score baseline*

*It should be noted that the "catch and score" move requires that the post player obtain and hold position that will allow the post player to catch the ball and score.

Perimeter Moves*

Go to move:
3-point shot
3-point shot
3-point shot
Drive to the goal
Shot fake and drive

Counter move:
Drive to the goal in one dribble
Shot fake and drive to the goal
Shot fake and mid-range shot
3-point shot
3-point shot

*It should be noted that the best weapon the outside shooter can have is a penetration game. The best weapon the penetrator can have is an outside shot.

More Lagniappe
The Shooting Progression

Shadow Shooting: Players partner up with a ball at a goal. More than one group may shoot at a goal. The ball is placed on the court and players take turn "shadow shooting" without a ball. The partner who is not shooting watches and makes suggestions about possible corrections in technique for their shooting partner. Two or three repetitions each are enough for daily practice. By shooting the ball to one another, the focus is on technique and not making the basket. Players are to hold a high, one-second follow through.

Shadow Shooting With a Ball: The second step in the shooting progression is for the players to pick up their ball and shoot the ball to one another. For their target, the players should focus on the piece of the court in between their partner's feet. The partner should allow the ball to strike the court if possible. Again, the partner's offer constructive criticism if needed while shadow shooting with a ball. The shooters should shoot the ball as high as the top of the backboard while performing this exercise. Like shadow shooting without a ball, two or three repetitions are sufficient for daily practice. Players are to hold a high, one-second follow through.

Straight Line Shooting: The focus of this portion of the shooting progression is shooting the ball on a "shot line." While this can be done against a wall or any flat surface so the ball will rebound directly back to the shooter, the idea surface is the edge of the backboard as shown in the photograph above and to the right. Players like the challenge of shooting the ball against the edge of the backboard. Failure to do so will result in the ball rebounding at an unusual angle, letting the player know the ball did not follow a straight shot line.

By not concentrating on "making the basket" the shooter focuses on keeping the ball straight and developing the techniques necessary to have a consistently straight shot line. Players are to hold a high, one-second follow through.

Green Light Shooting: Players like to come into the gym and immediately begin launching 3-point shot attempts. If the first shot goes in the player often thinks, "this is going to be a good shooting day!" If the first shot is missed, the player will often think the opposite, "this is going to be a bad shooting day!" The truth is the how the brain perceives things will go that day will often play a role in the success or failure of the shooter that practice or game.

The purpose of Green Light Shooting is to both warm up the shot while working on good shooting technique and to have immediate success shooting, helping the brain to think this session will be a successful one.

The first partner makes 20 shots from 2-3 feet from the goal. The shots should be clean swishes with no iron or backboard. The partner rebounds. After the first partner has made 20 shots, the second partner shoots. Both shooters work their way around the goal in a semi-circle and then back to their starting point. For post players an exception can be made and all 20 of the shots are bank shots.

If only one drill in the entire shooting progression can be done on a daily basis in practice, this is the drill to use. Players still hold a high one-second follow through and coach each other while doing Green Light Shooting.

Grooving the Shot: Grooving the shot is the most time consuming portion of the shooting progression. The first shooter takes a shot from three feet in front of the rim. If the shooter swishes the shot, makes it cleanly with no rim or backboard, the shooter takes one large step backwards.

If the shooter misses the shot, the shooter takes a step forward. If the shooter makes the shot, but not cleanly, the shooter takes another shot from the exact same spot.

The shooter works his or her way back in a straight line from the goal until he or she has reached his or her maximum range. The partner then repeats the process while the first shooter rebounds.

The ideal location is directly in front of the rim. If there are too many groups of shooters for each group to use this location, working from the baseline or at a 45-degree angle are fine, simply insist the shooters work in a straight line as they work their way to the maximum of their shooting range.

Even More Lagniappe!

The following is an excerpt from the book *Fine Tuning Your Zone Attack Offense.*

10

The Mental Approach to Attacking a Zone Defense

Number 1
Be Assertive and Confident

Zone defense, even when a strength for the opponent, has weaknesses capable of being exploited. An offensive unit should view every zone defense as an opportunity to be exploited and taken advantage of.

Zone defenses by their very nature want to cause the opponent to become passive on offense. Zone defense, even aggressive zones, should be attacked! Refer to zone offense as zone attack!

Knowing how to identify the weak points of a zone and how to exploit these weaknesses will breed confidence in offensive play. Teaching players to be assertive against a zone and to attack will prevent a passive approach to zone offense.

Number 2
Identify the Zone as Quickly as Possible

In order to be confident and assertive in attacking any zone defense, the offense must identify the form of zone defense being played. This is essential in order for the appropriate tactics and concepts to be used to attack the zone at its weak points.

Number 3
Identify the Weakness of the Zone and Attack

Identify the weak points of the zone and attack. All zones have weak points. There is some variation in these weak points due to slight variations in how a defensive unit plays the zone or the personnel being utilized.

Teams must have a plan to test the normal weak points of the specific zone being played and have an idea of how to identify and recognize the weak points.

Number 4
Identify the Weakest Defender in the
Zone and Attack

In addition to identifying the weak points in a zone defense, it is essential to determine if a weak defender and what position the weak defender is playing in the zone.

Upon identifying the weak link defender, this defender should be attacked in as many different ways as possible by the offense. The goal should be to not only score as many times as possible but to force the opponent to change defenses or move the weak defender to another spot in the zone allowing other parts of the zone to be attacked.

Number 5
Think in Terms of Principles of Attack

Zone offenses are pre-determined patterns or continuities while other zone offenses are motion oriented. Regardless of the type of zone offense, all need to be flexible enough to allow adaptation to attack the differences and variations in zone defenses.

This flexibility allows specific principles to be applied in attacking the weak points of a zone defense. The offense should think in terms of how every zone defense it faces can be attacked, which principles and tactics should be used to attack and how to apply the principles in attacking the defense.

11

Zone Attack Principles

Principles of attacking a zone defense can be categorized in order to organize the concepts, making the information easier for both coaches and players to utilize. The seven categories of zone attack principles are:

- Spacing and gaps
- Move the ball and move people
- Penetration
- Use of the dribble to attack
- Screen the zone
- The inside game against the zone
- Planning to rebound and floor balance

Spacing and gaps are concepts having to do with taking advantage of natural gaps in the zone defense through the use of proper spacing of offensive players and using alignments to place offensive players in the gaps of the zone defense.

Move the ball and move people are concepts concerning how the offense flows, the ball is moved to advantage for the offense and moving offensive players to attack the zone defense. Often these two seemingly different movements are interconnected and considerable time and effort must be spent to coordinate the two successfully.

All defensive systems are vulnerable to penetration and the zone defense is no different. Concepts in this category concern penetration by a variety of means, not all of which involve the use of the dribble to penetrate.

The use of the dribble as an offensive weapon is one of the must misunderstood and misused of all offensive weapons. Players and coaches tend to think of the dribble as a means to attack for a score. Against a zone, the dribble is a tool to attack the zone to set up the score.

One of the most effective weapons against man-to-man defense is the screen. This excellent offensive tool, when combined with ball movement and player movement is one of the most difficult offensive weapons for man-to-man defense to defend. Yet this same concept is seldom applied against a zone defense. The screen, when combined with ball and player movement, is one of the most effective concepts available to attack a zone defense.

Zone defenses were often created to defend against great inside offensive players and are still effective in that role. Many teams when confronted with a zone defense abandon any serious attempt to enter the ball into the post, either high or low, and resort to utilizing only mid-range jump shots or the three-point shot as a means of attacking the zone. Sadly, with simple concepts and principles, it can be easier to enter the ball into the post against a zone than against a good man-to-man defense.

One of the arguments against zone defenses is zones are weak against the offensive rebound due to the fact the defenders do not have individual block out assignments. This is true for poorly coached zone defenses but well coached zone defenses have specified rebounding schemes and are quite effective in limiting offensive rebound opportunities.

One of the best ways to obtain high percentage shots and draw fouls is by obtaining offensive rebounds. Many zone offenses are weak in the area of planning to position for offensive rebound opportunities.

During this phase of the offense, when neither team is in possession of the ball, it is essential the offense prepare for the likelihood of having to make defensive transition. The zone offense must have a scheme for balancing the floor on a shot attempt to prevent the opponent from fast breaking and to begin the transition to defense.

12

Spacing and Gaps

Number 6
Proper Spacing is Essential

Spacing is offense and offense is spacing. All players must be 15 to 18 feet apart. Correct spacing prevents the zone from being able to utilize one defensive player to defend two offensive players in one area.

Number 7
Constantly Readjust Spacing

As the offense attacks the zone and players move spacing must be maintained and players must be aware of the need to maintain, and if necessary, adjust spacing in order to prevent the defense from being able to use one defender to guard two offensive players.

Number 8
Stretch the Zone From Behind

Zone defenses want to defend as little area of the court as possible. The further from the goal the zone offense initiates its attack, the less area the zone has to defend (**Diagram 8-A**).

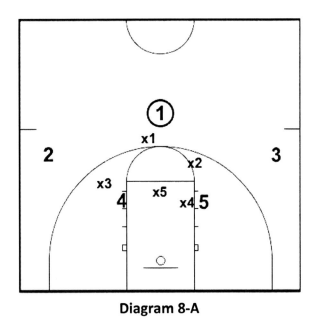

Diagram 8-A

Moving the post players deep behind the zone defense forces the zone to defend a greater area of the court, creating larger gaps in the zone for the offense to exploit (**Diagram 8-B**).

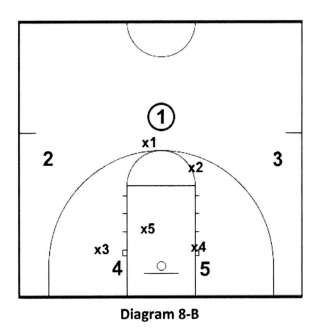

Diagram 8-B

Number 9
Flash Into Gaps

Zone defenses by their very nature have "gaps" in the defense. A gap is the space between two defenders in the zone. Cutters can exploit gaps by flashing into the gaps, particularly from behind the zone.

This tactic is effective due to the space between the defenders and the fact all five zone defenders will usually be focused on the ball by design (**Diagram 9-A and 9-B**).

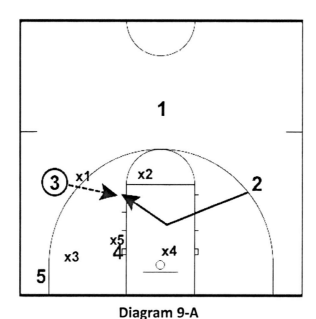

Diagram 9-A

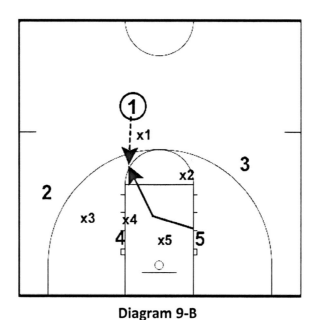

Diagram 9-B

Other Books by Coach Sivils

Game Strategy and Tactics for Basketball: Bench Coaching for Success

The Game of Basketball: Basketball Fundamentals, Intangibles and Finer Points of the Game for Coaches, Players and Fans

Better Basketball Practices

Goal Setting for Sport: A Concise Guide for Coaches and Athletes

From the Fine Tuning Series:

Fine Tuning Your Fast Break

Fine Tuning Your Man-to-Man Defense

Fine Tuning Your Zone Attack Offense

Available as Kindle Editions:

Game Strategy and Tactics for Basketball: Bench Coaching for Success

The Game of Basketball: Basketball Fundamentals, Intangibles and Finer Points of the Game for Coaches, Players and Fans

Better Basketball Practices

Goal Setting for Sport: A Concise Guide for Coaches and Players

Fine Tuning Your Fast Break

Fine Tuning Your Man-to-Man Defense

Fine Tuning Your Zone Attack Offense

Available from Amazon as paperback or Kindle Editions.
Also available from Barnes and Noble, Sysko's Sports and KCS Basketball.

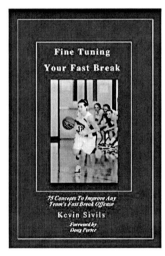

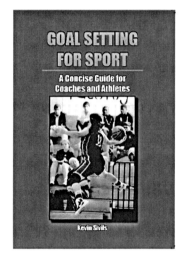

CPSIA information can be obtained
at www.ICGtesting.com
Printed in the USA
LVOW09s1312101017
551887LV00012B/158/P

9 781469 919164